Regarding the Front Cover

The depiction on the front cover is that of Sisyphus, the King of Corinth in Greek mythology.

> The gods had condemned Sisyphus to ceaselessly rolling a rock to the top of a mountain, where the stone would fall back of its own weight. They had thought with some reason that there is no more dreadful punishment than futile and hopeless labor.
> - Albert Camus, *The Myth of Sisyphus*

However, Sisyphus bears his fate and scorns the gods who condemned him by not lamenting his task. He persists at his labor, thus showing himself superior to the gods who sentenced him. Camus is not alone in his estimation of Sisyphus as a heroic figure.

Be not afraid of greatness: some are born great, some achieve greatness, and some have greatness thrust upon them.
William Shakespeare, *Twelfth Night* (2.1.156 -159)

Heroism as Virtue

Reflecting on Human Greatness

Max Malikow

Heroism as Virtue

Copyright © 2017 by Max Malikow

Published by: Theocentric Publishing
1069A Main Street
Chipley, Florida 32428

www.theocentricpublishing.com

Library of Congress Control Number 2018932106

ISBN 9780998560663

Dedications

To Rachel Joy Goodman: Who has shown resilience this past year amidst pain and frustration while maintaining her irrepressible sense of humor.

To Thomas Lickona: Who believes character matters and has devoted his professional life accordingly.

To Evelyn Malikow: Who has suffered heartbreaking losses with strength and grace without bitterness.

To Diane: Who is ineffably kind to everyone she encounters.

Acknowledgments

Writing an acknowledgment is an odd type of writing because it's the part of a book few people read. Nevertheless, I enjoy writing them because they mark the end of a writing project. (I save the acknowledgment for last.) More important, they remind me the work of writing, which seems solitary, actually is not.

This book would not have been written except for Rabbi Dr. Michael Kagan and Rabbi Dr. Earl Grollman. My attention was first drawn to the subject of heroism when I became curious about the course "Heroism and the Human Spirit" taught by Professor Kagan at LeMoyne College.

Nearly 20 years ago Earl Grollman mentored me in writing my first book, something I could not have done without his encouragement and guidance. Because of him I have learned the satisfaction and growth that derives from the hard work of writing.

Preface

On a normal day, we value heroism because it is uncommon. On September 11, we valued heroism because it was everywhere.

Nancy Gibbs

Anyone who does anything to help a child in his life is a hero to me.

Fred Rogers

This book began in the spring of 2015 when LeMoyne College Philosophy Department Chair, C. Tabor Fisher, asked if I would be willing to teach "Heroism and the Human Spirit" (PHL 403). Having taught this course previously, I spent the summer organizing my notes and reading further on the subject of heroism. But occasion and opportunity do not justify the existence of a book; neither do they provide sufficient motivation for a writing project.

Novelists are inspired by a determination to create and convey a story worth telling. Nonfiction writers are motivated by the conviction that a new idea is worthy of written expression or an existing idea is ripe for further development or refinement. The book you are about to read (if you so decide) is the result of my observation that heroism is so fascinating a topic that we never tire of heroic stories, either fictional or real-life.

Stories of heroic acts get our attention, making us wish to be more heroic in our own lives. John Keats wrote of the electric fire in human nature that gives birth to heroism and Albert Camus characterized heroism as accessible to all of us. More recently, Philip Zombardo, a psychology professor, expressed a desire to democratize heroism through his teaching. While preparing the aforementioned course it occurred to me that a written version of the course's numerous heroic instantiations might have the good effect of going beyond my students, making others aware of their potential for heroism. I agree with the novelist Jodi Picoult's expanded understanding of heroism:

> Heroes didn't leap tall buildings or stop bullets with an outstretched hand; they didn't wear boots and capes. They bled, and they bruised, and their superpowers were as simple as listening, or loving. Heroes were ordinary people who knew that even if their own lives were impossibly knotted, they could untangle someone else's (2017).

Max Malikow
Syracuse, NY
July 12, 2017

Table of Contents

I. What Is Heroism and Why Do We Admire Heroes?

I have seen the moment of my greatness flicker, And I have seen the eternal Footman hold my coat, and snicker, And, in short, I was afraid.

"The Love Song of J. Alfred Prufrock," T.S. Eliot

Heroes are not born, they are cornered.

Anonymous

In *Everyday Morality*, philosophy professor Mike W. Martin describes this terrifying episode.

In a wilderness area in a city where I live, a woman was hiking with her five-year-old daughter in 1986. A mountain lion attacked the girl and dragged her into some bushes. The mother's frantic screams were heard by Gregory Ysais, a thirty-six-year-old electronics technician who happened to be hiking in the same area. Without any hesitation Ysais ran to the scene to find the cougar gripping the bloody and squirming child by the back of her neck. Ysais grabbed a branch and repeatedly swung it over the cougar's head. The full-grown cougar responded with threatening roars and quick strikes with his huge paws. After a few minutes the cougar dropped the child long enough for her to be pulled away.

Ysais later reported that he had never been in a life-and-death situation before and had never thought of himself as a hero: "I didn't give it much thought. I just heard people crying for help, and I just ran as fast as I could. I was just doing what I had to do. I couldn't think of anything else" (1986, p. 121).

Although he did not recognize the danger to himself, calculate the risk, and consider the option of avoidance most people would consider Greg Ysais a hero. Even if he does not think of himself as a hero, most people would like to believe they would have acted as he did.

Determining what constitutes heroism requires first considering several questions: How is "hero" defined? What are the characteristics that distinguish a hero from a non-hero? Does a single heroic act make a person a hero? Are people heroes if they acted in the line of duty or in response to a calling? Does heroism require the elements of choice and/or overcoming fear? Is it possible to be heroic while living a mundane, unrecognized life?

How is "hero" defined?

The *American Heritage Dictionary* offers six definitions of hero, two of which are not relevant to this book: "a sandwich of heroic size made with a small loaf of crusty bread split lengthwise, containing lettuce, condiments, and a variety of meats and cheeses" and "any male regarded as a potential lover or protector" (my apologies to Subway and Olive Oyl's Popeye). The four remaining definitions are relevant to the matter at hand; they refer to mythology, courage, fiction, and accomplishment (1973, pp. 617-618).

In mythology and legend a hero is a being, often born of one mortal and one divine parent, who is favored by the gods, endowed with great courage and strength, and celebrated for bold exploits. Achilles embodies this definition. In *The Iliad*, he ponders the glory that will be his if he remains in Troy and fights in the Trojan War. This glory, however, will be at the expense of his life. (The Greek word for "glory" is *kleos*, the fame which is often heard through a song or poem.)

> My mother Thetis tells me there are two ways in which I may meet my end. If I stay here and fight then I shall lose my safe homecoming but I will have glory that is unwilting. Whereas if I go home my glory will die, but it will be a long time before the outcome of death shall take me (Homer, 1998, 9.410-416).

Perhaps the most common understanding of a hero is one who is noted for feats of courage or nobility of purpose, especially at the risk or sacrifice of life. The aforementioned Gregory Ysais fits this description as does the unnamed pilot in Kay Jamison's memoir, *An Unquiet Mind*. Faced with the dilemma of parachuting from his malfunctioning jet to safety or staying with the plane and guiding it away from a schoolyard full of children, he chose the latter and died in a fiery crash.

A familiar use of the word hero is "the principle character in a novel, poem, or dramatic presentation" (*American Heritage Dictionary*, 1973, p. 617). A Victor Hugo character, Jean Valjean in *Les Miserables,* is one of countless literary and theatrical protagonists who fits this characterization (1987).

Individuals of noteworthy achievement often are referred to as heroes. Babe Ruth in baseball, Muhammed Ali in boxing, and the Rev. Dr. Martin Luther King, Jr. in civil rights are men of accomplishment who enjoy heroic status.

What are the characteristics of a hero?

How is a hero distinguished from a non-hero? In situations that call for heroic action, are there only two possibilities for those in a position to respond? Returning to Gregory Ysais,

3

was he in a situation in which he was going to be either a hero or coward? He acted heroically, but would he have been a coward had he not intervened? Were there only two options available to him: either engage the mountain lion or allow the animal to have its way with the child without interference? Had Ysais stood by and watched the outcome for the girl would have been the same as if he had walked away from the horrific scene. Further, if he had not intervened, would he be a villain, even though he was not the one harming the child?

Shakespeare wrote, "Be not afraid of greatness: some are born great, some achieve greatness, and some have greatness thrust upon them" (*Twelfth Night*, 2.1.156-159). Ysais, not seeking an opportunity to act heroically, had greatness thrust upon him. He came upon a crisis and reacted in an exemplary manner. (Interesting is the Mandarin Chinese characters that combine to be translated *crisis* in English are "danger" and "opportunity.")

Certainly, anyone who orchestrated a situation for the purpose of acquiring heroic status would not be a hero. An episode of a television program of many years ago, "Hill Street Blues," featured a police officer who had accidentally shot and killed a little boy. Guilt-ridden and disgraced, he seemed to have made a start at restoring his soiled reputation when he rescued a child from a burning house. When it was discovered that he had arranged for the fire to create an opportunity for heroism his ignominy became even greater.

Does a single act of heroism make a person a hero?

In *Out of Character* psychologists David DeSteno and Pierrecarlo Valdesolo express curiosity about the disproportionate power of a bad deed to "erase a lifetime of good behavior" while a good deed is incapable of eradicating a lifetime of bad behavior (2013, p. 6).

Why does a single moral failing seem to give us license to brand someone with an indelible mark of bad character? One explanation is that these single events are so shocking and so memorable (not to mention so beat to death by the media), they eclipse all else. But if you buy that view, then why isn't the reverse true? Why doesn't a single good deed, even a memorable one, ever seem to be seen as a mark capable of defining a person's true colors? (pp. 6-7).

One of the ways in which we can know ourselves is to consider who we are most of the time. Heroic is but one of 17,953 personality traits (Allport, 1936). Unlike heroic, traits like patient, self-disciplined, and generous can be demonstrated daily. Occasions to act heroically are few and many people never encounter even one opportunity for a flickering moment of greatness, let alone fifteen minutes of fame.

One way to consider the sufficiency of a single courageous act to establish someone as a hero is to ponder if an opportunity generates heroism or elicits it. In *The Wizard of Oz*, the Cowardly Lion entering the witch's castle to rescue Dorothy did not create courage in the faltering lion (Baum, 2000). Rather, Dorothy's abduction provided the opportunity for the lion's dormant courage to be activated. The lyrics from the song "Tin Man" include an analysis that also applies to the lion: "Oz never did nothing to the tin man, that he didn't already have" (Bunnell, 2000). This assessment suggests there are people who never encounter a situation that would awaken their latent courage, implying there are many unrealized heroes among us.

This is not to say courage cannot be developed. Courage often involves the subordination of fear to duty and nearly always demands doing the more difficult thing. This means courage requires self-discipline, a trait that can be nurtured.

The noted biologist Thomas Huxley was so convinced of this he wrote: "The chief purpose of education is to train a person to do what he ought to do, when it ought to be done, whether he feels like it or not" (Wheelock, 1910, p. 33). If the potential for heroism resides in someone, it is because of internalized values that enable the recognition of things that have greater worth than comfort, safety, and, in rare circumstances, self-preservation. Heroes are those whose well-developed self-discipline and discernment enable them to rise to the occasion when courage is summoned. On such occasions courage is the by-product of self-discipline, values, and a moral code that have developed over time.

"Assume a virtue, if you have it not," wrote Shakespeare (4.4.162). There are virtues that can be feigned, but courage is not one of them. Brave and noble deeds are empirical demonstrations of courage; without courage there would be no courageous acts. For this reason, a single, heroic act is sufficient to qualify an individual as a hero.

Nevertheless, it is reasonable to ask if subsequent failures of courage call for an individual's reclassification as a coward. An inspirational song asks for, "one moment in time when I'm more than I thought I could be" (Hammond and Bettis, 1988). As previously stated, we are who we are most of the time. Notwithstanding, it is also true that we are who we are in our best moments. These characterizations are not contradictory. No single maxim can capture the essence of any human being, many are needed. Each one provides a perspective. If just once we have exceeded our self-perceived capability, we have been that person, if only for one moment in time. A new standard of excellence has been established and with it higher expectations, as well as an increased probability for disappointment.

Are people heroes if they acted in the line of duty or in response to a calling?

On January 15, 2009 U.S. Airways pilot Chesney "Sully" Sullenberger landed airliner flight 1549 on the Hudson River after a flock of birds collided with the plane, disabling both engines. One-hundred and fifty-five passengers were grateful for this unconventional landing. It would seem odd to question Captain Sullenberger's status as a national hero on the ground that safely landing airplanes is part of his job description. Similarly, it would seem odd, actually ludicrous, to question if firefighters who entered the World Trade Center towers on September 11, 2001 are heroes since entering burning buildings is what firefighters are supposed to do.

"People keep telling me it was a heroic thing to do. In my opinion it was just the right thing to do" (Hartsock, 05/10/10). These are the words of Dave Hartsock, a skydiving instructor who was strapped to his student, Shirley Dygert, in what is called a tandem jump. (Tandem jumps are used in a first jump experience.) When their first parachute opened partially and the reserve chute became entangled in the first one, instructor and student went into a death spiral at 10,000 feet. At 500 feet and descending at 40 miles per hour, Hartsock skillfully managed the control toggles and rotated his body under Dygert's so he would serve as a cushion to reduce the impact of her fall. He is now a quadriplegic with only slight movement in his right arm. Hartsock does not think of himself as a hero. "I was the one who was completely responsible for her safety. What other choices were there?" (05/10/10).

In 1956, Christian missionary Jim Eliot and four of his associates were slain by Waudani tribesman in Ecuador. The five men were speared to death by the very people to whom they believe they had been sent to present the gospel of Jesus Christ. By virtue of their ultimate sacrifice, these missionaries are martyrs, heroes of the Christian faith. Nobel laureate Mother Teresa of Calcutta, canonized as a saint in 2016, also carried on her work in response to a calling, thereby sacrificing whatever other life she might have had. These missionaries and Mother Teresa did their work neither as a job nor a profession, but in obedience to a calling. However admirable such obedience might be, can it be considered heroic if it is compelled by a divine directive?

Merely doing one's job or carrying out a divinely inspired mission is heroic when the accomplishment is extraordinary or the sacrifice is great. Captain Sullenberger was trained and hired to land airplanes on runways - not rivers. The firefighters who entered the towers of the World Trade Center were trained for extinguishing fires and making rescues in a variety of situations, but not the one that confronted them on 9/11. Jim Eliot, his fellow missionaries, and Mother Teresa embodied extraordinary faith in the One who called them to serve.

Does heroism require the elements of choice and/or overcoming fear?

Aristotle's Principle of the Golden Mean characterizes a virtue as the apex between two extremes, both of which are vices. From this construction, the virtue of courage is the zenith between the vices of recklessness and cowardice. Recklessness is expressed by action without an appreciation of danger.

Without the recognition of danger, there can be no experience of fear. Inaction resulting from the awareness of danger is cowardice. The Aristotilian concept of courage requires action despite fear. The application of the Principle of the Golden Mean to courage gives rise to two questions: Is an action heroic if it did not require overcoming fear? And, is an action heroic if there was no choice but to act? Gregory Ysais said he intervened without thinking, making his action more a reflex rather than a deliberate act. Since he acted without recognizing the danger or considering the option of non-involvement his action does not conform to Aristotle's formula for courage. Similarly, it could be argued that Islamic jihadist suicide bombers and World War II Japanese kamikaze pilots cannot be heroes since their cultural conditioning precluded authentic choice-making. It is not always clear whether someone actually has a choice. Did Aron Ralston, the trapped mountain climber who amputated his arm rather than die in a cave, really have a choice? His options were to remain pinned until he died an agonizing death from starvation or experience the ineffable pain of removing his arm with a utility knife. Is it any wonder the title of his memoir is *Between a Rock and a Hard Place* (2004)?

Individuals who subordinated fear or endured pain to achieve something perceived of greater value have acted commendably, if not heroically. This being said, people also can act heroically without confronting fear or the possibility of avoidance. Reconsider Ysais and Ralston and ask, "Could I have done that?" If your answer is, "I don't think so," or "I don't know, but I would hope so," or "No, but I admire what they did," then this is sufficient to establish them as heroic. Of course, this is a sentimentalist argument. (Sentimentalism is the belief that some knowledge cannot be acquired from reason or scientific demonstration, but only from the feeling that something is true.) The counter to this would be a logical argument, perhaps in the form of a syllogism:

> Major Premise
> All heroic acts include the
> subordination of fear and/or
> option of avoidance.
> Minor Premise
> Ysais fighting off a mountain lion
> included neither subordination of
> fear nor the option of avoidance.
> Conclusion
> Therefore, Ysais did not engage in a

an act of heroism.

The flaw in this syllogism resides in the major premise. While it could be argued that all subordination of fear is a demonstration of heroism, it does not follow that all acts of heroism include the subordination of fear. (The same can be said about the option of avoidance.)

Stanford University psychologist Philip Zimbardo, founder of the Heroic Imagination Project, believes if sociopaths are the result of nurturing it follows that heroes can be developed as well:

> We have been saddled too long with (a) mystical view of heroism. We assume heroes are demigods. But they're not. A hero is just an ordinary person who does something extraordinary. I believe we can use science to teach people how to do that (Lehrer, 2010).

Is it possible to be a hero living an ordinary, unrecognized life?

It is not typical of scholarship to buttress a philosophical position by citing a professional athlete. However, an observation made by basketball superstar Charles Barkley is relevant to the question of whether an ordinary, unpublicized person can be a hero. In the wake of the revelation of National Football League quarterback Michael Vick's dog-fighting fiasco, Barkley challenged the assumption that athletes are role models: "Just because I dunk a basketball doesn't mean I should raise your kids" (12/25/10). He vehemently denied that he, Michael Vick, Michael Jordan or any other sports celebrity is a hero or role model for children. Barkley posits each father bears this responsibility for his own children. Zimbardo agrees with Barkley: "One of the problems with our culture is that we've replaced heroes with celebrities. We worship people who haven't done anything" (Lehrer, 2010).

For some, a philosophical position articulated by Charles Barkley does not carry sufficient weight to be convincing. (Anyone who has seen Barkley would recognize him as a man who carries considerable weight.) Such an objection, however, would be an *ad hominem* argument. Heroism is expressed moment-by-moment all over the world when extraordinary, unpublicized acts of virtue occur. This opinion does not devalue heroism, rather it elevates it to something anyone can do, perhaps even frequently.

Why do we admire heroes?

Why are heroes universally admired? Why are they a source of fascination as well as inspiration for virtually everyone? Might it be that heroes remind us of our potential, challenging us to consider capabilities we want to believe we have - and just might? The renowned social philosopher Eric Hoffer recognized this possibility and wrote:

> The capacity for identifying with others seems boundless. No matter how meagerly endowed, we find it easy to identify ourselves with persons of exceptional endowments or achievements. Can it be that even in the least of us there are crumbs of abilities and potentialities so that we can comprehend greatness as if it were part of us? (1973, p. 82).

Similarly, in his Pulitzer Prize winning collection of short biographies, *Profiles in Courage*, John Kennedy spoke of heroism with a caveat: "The stories of past courage can define that ingredient - they can teach, they can offer hope, they can provide inspiration. But they cannot supply courage. For this each man must look into his own soul" (1957, p. 225).

Heroes encourage the belief that even if God does not exist the world can be a better place because of certain people. One of the best known studies in psychological history is Stanley Milgram's "Obedience and Compliance Experiment," which revealed a dark and disheartening aspect of the human condition. In the experiment, human subjects administered electrical shocks to people simply because they were told to dispense the shocks. Zimbardo, who believes heroism can be taught, offers an optimistic assessment:

> Just look at the Milgram experiment. Everybody uses that as an example of how bad people are. But the actual data are not so depressing. If subjects watched someone else refuse to issue shocks, then they almost always refused to do so, too. The hero created another hero (Lehrer, 2010).

Mark Twain believed heroes do things we admit we cannot do. He wrote, "We find not much in ourselves we admire, we are always privately wanting to be like someone else. If everybody was satisfied with himself, there would be no heroes" (2015). His view implies heroism is not contagious. William Kilpatrick and David Brooks, two contemporary writers, disagree with Twain. The former has written:

> Stories help make sense of our lives. They also create a desire to be good. Plato, who thought long and hard about the subject of moral education, believed that children should be brought up in such a way that they would fall in love with virtue. And he thought that stories and histories were the key to sparking this desire. No amount of discussion or dialogue could compensate if that spark was missing (1992, p. 27).

The latter believes, "we can immerse ourselves in the lives of outstanding people and try to understand the wisdom of the way they lived. ... and emerge slightly different and slightly better" (2015, p. 15).

Heroic stories are discoverable in every culture and every era. They provide compelling evidence that people believe, and have always believed, they can improve themselves and, thereby, make the world a better place even in the absence of a divine being or mythical superheroes.

heroism, virtue, and circumstances

Areteology, the study virtue, derives from the Greek *arete*, defined as "goodness, excellence of any kind" (Liddell and Scott, 2017). In this book heroism is treated as the extraordinary expression of one or more of nine virtues. The sources from which these virtues were drawn are the four *cardinal virtues* of classical antiquity, the six *core values* of Martin Seligman and Chris Peterson (2004), and three virtues from my own research. The *cardinal virtues* (courage, self-control, justice, and wisdom) are a subset of the *core values*, which also include "love for humanity" and "spirituality and transcendence." To these six I added integrity, perseverance, and resilience.

In addition to these nine virtues, heroism is considered in the context of five circumstances:

> conflicting obligations
> commitment and sacrifice
> redemption
> self-awareness and change
> facing death

Since it is not unusual for heroism to demonstrate more than one virtue, some instances of heroism will be referred to in more than one of the following chapters.

II. Heroism as Courage

I wanted you to see what real courage is, instead of getting the idea that courage is a man with a gun in his hand. It's when you know you're licked before you begin, but you begin anyway and see it through no matter what.

Harper Lee

Courage doesn't always roar. Sometimes courage is the quiet voice at the end of the day saying, "I will try again tomorrow."

Mary Ann Radmacher

Aristotle characterized moral excellence as "a state concerned with choice (and) ... a mean between two vices" (1984, p. 1748). Accordingly, he characterized courage as the tendency to do good in spite of fear and the wise balance between the vices of recklessness and cowardice.

> *Courage* is feeling the correct amount of fear and confidence when acting in dangerous or difficult situations. Feeling too much fear and too little confidence is the vice of cowardice, while recklessness occurs when a person feels too little fear and too much confidence (Birsch, 2014, p. 158).

"The Princess Diaries," a movie based on Meg Cabot's novel of the same name, provides a similar description of courage: "Courage is not the absence of fear, but rather the judgment that something else is more important than fear. The brave may not live forever, but the cautious do not live at all" (2001).

British Prime Minister Harold Wilson said, "Courage is the art of being the only one who knows you're scared to death" (2015). This seems to have been the experience of Lutheran minister Dietrich Bonhoeffer when confined in a Nazi concentration camp because of his public opposition to Adolf Hitler. Silence would have prevented Bonhoeffer's imprisonment and eventual execution, but he believed, "The only thing necessary for the triumph of evil is for good men to do nothing" (Burke, 2015). One month before his hanging he wrote a reflective poem titled, "Who Am I?"

> Who am I? They often tell me,
> I come out of my cell's confinement
> calmly, cheerfully, firmly,
> like a squire from his country-house.
>
> Who am I? They often tell me,
> I would talk to my warders
> freely and friendly and clearly,
> as though it were mine to command.
>
> Who am I? They also tell me
> I would bear the days of misfortune
> equably, smilingly, proudly,
> like one accustomed to win.
>
> Am I really all that which other men tell of?
> Or am I only what I know of myself?
> restless and longing and sick, like a bird in a cage,
> struggling for breath, as though hands were compressing my throat, yearning for colors, for flowers, for the voices of birds, thirsty for words of kindness, for neighborliness, trembling in expectation of great events, powerlessly trembling for friends at an infinite distance, weary and empty at praying, at thinking, at making, faint, and ready to say farewell to it all?

Who am I? This or the other?
Am I one person today, and tomorrow another?
Am I both at once? A hypocrite before others,
and before myself a contemptibly woebegone
weakling? Or is something within me still like a beaten
army, fleeing in disorder from a victory already
achieved?

Who am I? They mock me, these lonely questions of
mine.
Whoever I am, Thou knowest, O God, I am Thine
(1953, pp. 347-348).

Bonhoeffer's stand against the Nazi regime qualifies as courageous according to the criteria set forth by James Wallace. He considers an act courageous if it includes the recognition of danger, calculation of risk, option of avoidance, consensus of danger, absence of coercion, and self-control (1978, p.p. 78-81).

Another characterization of courage is that of Michael W. Martin, who believes courage can be displayed intermittently or singularly. Accordingly, he has written: "People are courageous if they either (1) show a tendency to do admirable acts in situations they see as dangerous or (2) act admirably to an extraordinary degree on one occasion, without acting cowardly on other occasions" (1989, p. 121). The heroic act of Gregory Ysais, recounted in the Introduction (p. 1), satisfies Martin's criteria. When Ysais confronted the mountain lion he engaged in an admirable act on a single occasion in a dangerous situation.

Courage in Battle

Easily recognized and frequently honored is courage on the battlefield. "The Congressional Medal of Honor is the highest award for valor in action against an enemy force which can be bestowed upon an individual serving in the Armed Services of the United States" (Congressional Medal of Honor Society, 2015). Concerning this award, it has been said, "You don't *win* the Medal of Honor, you *earn* it."

Soldiers in combat strive to comport themselves honorably. Certainly none of them want to demonstrate faintheartedness in battle. Cowardice, the antithesis of courage, is a manifestation of a weakness of will. "By definition, weakness of will involves a loss of self-control in the sense that we fail to guide our acts in the light of our values" (Martin, 1989, p. 124). This failure is powerfully portrayed in drama in the movie, "Courage Under Fire" (1996). Set in the Persian Gulf War, Sgt. John Monfriez, played by Lou Diamond Phillips, has a lapse in courage with a tragic consequence - the death of his superior officer. When an investigation reveals the truth of his cowardice in battle, he commits suicide.

What motivates courage?

To ask what motivates courage is to ask what accounts for strength of will. While an exhaustive list of incentives is an impossibility, there are at least four conditions that inspire courage: anger, duty, love, and survival.

anger

Slavery inflamed the anger of journalist and abolitionist William Loyd Garrison, who wrote,

I am aware that many object to the severity of my language; but is there not cause for severity? I will be as harsh as truth, and as uncompromising as justice. On this subject, I do not wish to think, or speak, or write, with moderation. ... urge me not to use moderation in a cause like the present. I am in earnest - I will not equivocate - I will not excuse - I will not retreat a single inch - and I will be heard. The apathy of the people is enough to make every statue leap from its pedestal, and to hasten the resurrection of the dead (1831).

Another abolitionist, John Brown, went beyond words and led armed insurrections in Kansas before his capture at Harper's Ferry, Virginia. On the day of his execution by hanging he handed a note to a guard that read: "I, John Brown, am now quite certain that the crimes of this guilty land will never be purged away but with blood. I had, as I now think, vainly flattered myself that without very much bloodshed it might be done" (2015).

Not everyone agrees that the Protestant Reformation was a positive movement. However, there is no denying that it required courage for its firebrand, Martin Luther, to stand against the Roman Catholic Church and Pope Leo X, who excommunicated him. Luther's anger toward the Church for its deviation from Scripture energized him for his monumental work.

> I find nothing that promotes work better than angry fervor. For when I wish to compose, write, pray and preach well, I must be angry. It refreshes my entire system, my mind is sharpened, and all unpleasant thoughts and depression fade away (2009, p. 110).

duty

Some heroism is motivated by a commitment to duty. Referred to in the Introduction are the altruistic suicide of an unnamed jet pilot and self-sacrificial heroism of David Hartsock, a skydiving instructor. A remarkable instantiation of heroism inspired by duty is that of Shoichi Yokoi, a World War II Japanese soldier who remained alone at his post until

1972, 27 years after the surrender of Japan. Yokoi was discovered in a jungle on the Island of Guam. His devotion is reminiscent of the irrepressible Black Knight, a fictional character in "Monty Python and the Holy Grail" (1975).

It is noteworthy that devotion to duty is neither courageous nor commendable when it is misguided. Several of the Nazi war criminals tried at Nuremberg for *crimes against humanity* argued for acquittal, claiming they were merely following orders. This argument was reactivated 30 years later when Lt. William Calley defended the killing of an estimated 400 civilians in the Vietnam War's infamous "My Lai Massacre." At his court martial he maintained he merely executed his assigned mission. (Lt. Calley is quoted at length in chapter X, "Heroism in Conflicting Obligations.")

love

Jesus taught, "Greater love has no one than this, that he lays down his life for his friends" (John 15:13, NIV). In the English language, the word *love* applies to a diversity of affections. In contrast, in Greek there are four words that can be translated as *love*. The word selected depends on the relationship between the lover and that which is loved. In Greek, s*torge* is the natural flow of affection parents have for their children; hence, it is sometimes spoken of as "motherly love." It was this love that motivated the heroic action reported in a *Washington Post* news story:

> Clementina Geraci, three months pregnant, made the decision of her life when doctors told her last spring that her breast cancer had spread. She could fight the cancer aggressively and have an abortion, or she could take less-hazardous cancer drugs and carry the baby to term. On Saturday, 4-month-old Dylan Geraci Winn

slept peacefully at his mother's funeral (Borgman, 1995).

A physician herself, Geraci fully understood her treatment options and the inherent risk in the choice she made.

Survival

In a strict linguistic sense, no human feat can be designated as "superhuman," since once something has been accomplished by someone it no longer exceeds human capability. Semantics notwithstanding, the lengths to which some people have gone to survive have provided stories that seem to cross the line that separates the credible from the incredible. Nando Parrado and Roberto Canessa's determination to live empowered them to an accomplishment that is mind-boggling as well as inspiring. Their survival story is reminiscent of Rudyard Kipling's classic poem, "If," that includes a description that applies to heroism:

> If you can force your heart and nerve and sinew
> To serve their turn long after they are gone,
> And so hold on when there is nothing left within you
> Except the will Which says to them "Hold on!"
> (11/19/2015)

Parrado and Canessa lived out this description in 1972 when they traversed 37 miles through the unforgiving terrain of the Andes following an airline crash. Untrained and unequipped for mountain climbing, they went for help in order to save their lives and the lives of fourteen other survivors of the crash. Weakened by nearly ten weeks of subsisting on scant provisions in frigid weather waiting for rescuers who were not coming, they completed an expedition that would have challenged even the most accomplished of mountaineers. Reflecting on his survival, Parrado offers this advice:

> As we used to say in the mountains, "Breathe. Breathe again. With every breath you are alive." After all these years, this is still the best advice I can give you: Savor your existence. Live every moment. Do not waste a breath (2015).

III. Heroism as Self-Discipline

I see my upbringing as a great success story. By disciplining me, my parents inculcated self-discipline. And by restricting my choices as a child, they gave me so many choices in my life as an adult. Because of what they did then, I get to do the work I love now.

Amy Chua

We all have dreams. But in order to make dreams come into reality, it takes an awful lot of determination, dedication, self-discipline, and effort.

Jesse Owens

Better a patient person than a warrior, one with self-control than one who takes a city.

Proverbs 16:32

One of the most memorable moments in Olympic Games history occurred in 1996 when an 18-year-old, 4'8" gymnast named Keri Strug completed her pommel horse vault by landing on a badly sprained ankle. The ankle had been severely injured in her previous vault. Courageous? Of course it was. Yet Strug's heroic, gold medal winning performance is even more impressive as a demonstration of self-discipline.

Self-discipline is the capacity for doing the harder thing, enabling an individual to do what ought to be done, when it ought to be done regardless of inhibiting feelings. Arguably, the impulse to avoid pain is the strongest inhibitor to human action. However, neuroscientist Robert Sapolsky has written about the effect of emotion on the brain's interpretation of and response to pain:

... the emotional/interpretive level can be dissociated from the objective amount of pain signal that is coursing up to the brain from the spine. In other words, how much pain you feel, and how unpleasant that pain feels, can be two separate things (2004, pp. 193-194).

When contemplating an action or resisting an impulse the brain's frontal cortex provides a menu of possible outcomes, as well as the probability of each. This assessment is followed by a question: *Are you certain you want to do this?* Imagine Keri Strug's frontal cortex operating at full-force while performing her vault, relentlessly informing her of the intense pain awaiting her when she would land on her injured ankle from a height exceeding her own. Further imagine the self-discipline required for her to stay on task, concentrating on her form while her frontal cortex was frantically advising her against what she was doing. The mind, the entity that directs mental processing, is capable of overruling the frontal cortex.

Temperance, an archaic term, is the characteristic of self-control. It enables restraint and moderation in action. Self-discipline, the dynamic equivalent of temperance, is featured in *The Road Less Traveled*, second only to the Bible as the all-time bestselling nonfiction book. Written by M. Scott Peck, a psychiatrist, he defined self-discipline as a composite of four attributes: "delaying of gratification, acceptance of responsibility, dedication to truth, and balancing" (1978, p. 18).

Another bestseller, *Emotional Intelligence: Why It Can Matter More Than IQ*, includes self-discipline as a necessary component for personal and professional success in life (1996). Its author, Daniel Goleman, defines self-discipline as a combination of *emotional management* and *motivation*. Concerning the former, he has written:

If your emotional abilities aren't in hand, if you don't have self-awareness, if you are not able to manage your distressing emotions, if you can't have empathy and have effective relationships, then no matter how smart you are, you are not going to get very far (2015).

Regarding motivation, Goleman agrees with the legendary football coach, Vince Lombardi, who said, "The only place success comes before work is in the dictionary" (2015).

The value of self-discipline is apparent from an exercise I have given my students over the years. I ask them to determine their proudest accomplishment and list the personality traits that made that accomplishment possible. Almost without exception, self-discipline is on that list. This is not surprising. According to Peck, "Discipline is the basic set of tools we require to solve life's problems" (1978, p. 15).

President Bill Clinton confessed to a lack of self-discipline when asked why he engaged in a dalliance with Monica Lewinsky: "I think I did something for the worst possible reason - just because I could. I think that's the most, just about the most morally indefensible reason that anybody could have for doing anything" (Rather, 06/20/2004). Plato's *Republic* includes a debate in which Plato's older brother, Glaucon, postulates a man will violate his own moral code if he is confident he can do so with impunity. Socrates voices his disagreement, arguing some men have sufficient integrity to restrain themselves from wrongdoing even when the risk of discovery and penalty are nonexistent. If President Clinton's explanation is to be understood as, "I thought I could get away with it," it shows not only a miscalculation on his part but support for Glaucon's assertion. In his view, the difference between just and unjust men is the probability of discovery and punishment. Socrates maintained there are intrinsically just men who are not slaves to their appetites and resist opportunities to misbehave, even when they could do so with impunity.

Sigmund Freud showed his appreciation for self-discipline with his characterization of adulthood as the ability to restrain impulses and postpone gratification: "Where id was, there shall be ego (2017). He believed maturity is reached when the id's (child's) drive for immediate gratification is restrained by the ego's (adult's) awareness of something more important than pleasure. A psychological study of delayed gratification was conducted by Walter Mischel in the late 1960's and early 1970's. He individually tested four and five-year-old children by placing them in a room with a marshmallow and instructing them that if they ate the marshmallow before he returned it would be the only marshmallow they would get. He also told them if they did not eat the marshmallow before he returned they could have a second one. (He left the room for 15 minutes.) Two follow-up studies, approximately 20 years later, showed children who did not eat the marshmallow before Mischel's return had academic and mental health histories more favorable than children who ate before his return.

This is not to assert that restraining from a tryst with a workplace subordinate or waiting before eating a marshmallow is heroic. Rather, it is to posit that self-discipline is one of the characteristics that can be expressed to a heroic degree. It is a trait nurtured over a lifetime. Just as a muscle grows incrementally as it is exercised, so also with self-discipline. Unlike height or eye color, temperance is not genetically transmitted. In addition to practice, self-discipline is derived from experience - the accumulation of real-life episodes from which one becomes convinced of its value and resolves to further develop it. A vexing feature of self-discipline is the feeling that it cannot be acquired without first having it. Two questions that might reinforce the value of self-discipline and its potential for energizing praiseworthy behavior are:

> (1) *Can you recall a time when you disappointed yourself?*

> (2) *If so, was this disappointment partially or entirely due to a failure of self-discipline?*

The virtues that manifest as heroism are often collaborative. Self-discipline not only enables perseverance but is reinforced by it. Andy Dufresne, the protagonist in Stephen King's novella, *Rita Hayworth and Shawshank Redemption*, is a man wrongfully sentenced to life imprisonment (1982). His escape plan took nearly 20 years to execute but his freedom was worth the effort and patience it required. Not only was self-discipline essential for accomplishing his escape, it enabled him to persevere through years of abuse.

A real-life demonstration of heroic self-discipline is the writing of *Cold Sassy Tree*, a bestselling novel by Olive Ann Burns (1984). Immediately after she was diagnosed with lymphoma she decided to write a novel in order to distract her from her illness. With her energy compromised by the disease and its treatment, it took eight-and-a-half years to complete the book. Her self-discipline enabled her to persevere through pain and fatigue to complete the project. The words of one her *Cold Sassy Tree* characters well describes her: "Like an actor whose audience has stood up to clap, I didn't want to quit" (1984, p. 174).

IV. Heroism as Justice

An injustice is tolerable only when it is necessary to avoid an even greater injustice.

John Rawls

He has showed you, O man, what is good. And what does the Lord require of you? To act justly and to love mercy and to walk humbly with your God.

Micah 6:8

The story of King Solomon's wise ruling in a seemingly impossible to resolve case is well-known beyond Israel, where it occurred, and well-known beyond readers of the Bible, where it is recorded. The case over which he adjudicated involved two women claiming the same infant boy.

> Now two prostitutes came before the king and stood before him. One of them said, "My lord, this woman and I live in the same house. I had a baby while she was there with me. The third day after my child was born, she also had a baby. We were alone; there was no one in the house but the two of us.
>
> During the night this woman's son died because she lay on him. So she got up in the middle of the night and she took my son from my side while I your servant was asleep. She put him by her breast and put her dead son by my breast. The next morning, I got up to nurse my son and he was dead. But when I looked at him closely in the morning light, I saw that it wasn't the son I had borne."
>
> The other woman said, "No! The living one is my son; the dead one is yours."

But the first one insisted, "No! The dead one is yours; the living one is mine." And so they argued before the king.

The king said, "This one says, 'My son is alive and your son is dead, while that one says, 'No! Your son is dead and mine is alive.' "

Then the king said, "Bring me a sword." So they brought a sword for the king. He then gave an order: "Cut the living child in two and give half to one and half to the other."

The woman whose son was alive was filled with compassion for her son and said to the king, "Please my lord, give her the living baby! Don't kill him!"

But the other said, "Neither I nor you shall have him. Cut him in two!"

Then the king gave this ruling: "Give the living baby to the first woman. Do not kill him, she is the mother" (1 Kings 3: 16-27).

Heroic justice occurs when an individual takes extraordinary action within the law to achieve an equitable result. Attributing the just result in this case to mere luck would be a misinterpretation of the story. The people recognized Solomon's ruling as an instance of heroic justice: "When all Israel heard the verdict the king had given, they held the king in awe because they saw he had wisdom from God to administer justice (1 Kings 3:28). An effect of Solomon's ruling is the confidence it gave the people of Israel that their king had God-given wisdom. This is what he prayed for when he succeeded his father, David, as king:

Now, O Lord my God, you have made your servant king in place of my father David. But I am only a little child and do not know how to carry my duties. Your servant is here among the people you have chosen, a great people too numerous to count or number. So give your servant a discerning heart to govern your people and to distinguish between right and wrong. For who is able to govern this great people of yours? (1 Kings 3: 7-9).

Justice is not a matter of simply adhering to the law. John Grisham's novel, *A Time to Kill*, is the story of a father who murdered the two men who abducted, raped, and savagely beat his ten-year-old daughter (1989). The drama in the story is the question of whether the jury will find it in their collective heart to acquit the father. As in the case that confronted Solomon, justice was a matter to be discerned by the heart rather than a statute. In the novel the father's defense attorney appealed to the jurors to ask themselves if it is reasonable and realistic to expect and require a loving father to restrain himself from avenging such evil.

Henry David Thoreau believed the law is not always in conformity with justice. In *Resistance to Civil Government* (a.k.a. *On Civil Disobedience*) he posited unjust laws exist and when they are encountered they should be disobeyed. He urged abolitionists not to pay taxes to any government that permits slavery, even if it means imprisonment. Accordingly, he wrote, "Under a government which imprisons any unjustly, the true place for a just man is also a prison" (2014, part 2.9).

Not surprising is Thoreau's influence on Mahatma Gandhi and the Rev. Dr. Martin Luther King, Jr. In his autobiography King wrote:

> During my student days I read Henry David Thoreau's essay *On Civil Disobedience* for the first time. Here, in this courageous New Englander's refusal to pay his taxes and his choice of jail rather than support a war that would spread slavery's territory into Mexico, I made my first contact with the theory of nonviolent

resistance. Fascinated by the idea of refusing to cooperate with an evil system, I was so deeply moved that I reread the work several times (1998, p. 14).

In "A Letter from Birmingham Jail" he distinguished *just* from *unjust* laws with these words:

A just law is a man-made code that squares with the moral law or the law of God. An unjust law is a code that is out of harmony with the moral law. Any law that uplifts human personality is just. Any law that degrades human personality is unjust (1989, p. 153).

In the same letter he addressed civil disobedience and one of its possible consequences:

One who breaks an unjust law must do so openly, lovingly, and with a willingness to accept the penalty. I submit that an individual who breaks a law that conscience tells him is unjust, and who willingly accepts the penalty of imprisonment in order to arouse the conscience of the community over its injustice, is in reality expressing the highest respect for the law (p. 153).

No sport has ever had a more academically accomplished commissioner than Major League Baseball when its Commissioner was A. Bartlett Giamatti. A Professor of English Renaissance Literature, he became the youngest President of Yale University, his alma mater, at the age of 40. However, his passion for baseball prevailed over his love for the academy and in 1986 he accepted the position of President of the National League, which he held for three years before his election as Commissioner of Major League Baseball. His untimely death from a heart attack five months later prematurely ended what likely would have been an exceptional tenure as professional baseball's chief executive. While serving as National League President, Giamatti ruled on an appeal made on behalf of Kevin Gross, a Philadelphia Phillies pitcher, who had attached a piece of sandpaper to his glove in order to secretively scuff the baseball. (Scuffing a ball affects its movement, making it more difficult to hit.) This was an unquestionable rule violation. Gross was ejected from the game and suspended for ten days. The suspension was appealed, requiring Giamatti to reconsider the suspension. Of his decision, he said,

> I worked as hard on my response to the Kevin Gross Appeal as I worked on anything I did while I was in New Haven (at Yale University). It was challenging to try to be clear about cheating and what it meant, and to be fair at the same time (Robson, 1998, p. 66).

The basis of the appeal was, "the ten-day suspension was unduly harsh; it was ... without precedent, inconsistent with past practices, and not comparable with discipline for other offenses" (p. 68). In his written decision, Giamatti brilliantly made a distinction between an act of premeditated cheating and a spontaneous loss of control.

> Such acts are not the result of impulse, born of frustration or anger or zeal, as violence is, but are rather acts of a cool, deliberate, premeditated kind. Unlike acts of impulse or violence, intended at the moment to vent frustration or abuse another, acts of cheating are intended to alter the very conditions of play to favor one person. They are secretive, covert acts that strike and seek to undermine the basic foundation of any contest declaring the winner - that all participants play under identical rules and

conditions. Acts of cheating destroy that necessary foundation and thus strike at the essence of a contest. They destroy faith in the game's integrity and fairness; if participants and spectators alike cannot assume integrity and fairness, and proceed from there, the contest in its essence cannot exist.

Acts of physical excess, reprehensible as they are, often represent extensions of the very forms of physical exertion that are the basis for playing the game; regulation and discipline seek to contain, not expunge, violent effort in sport. Cheating is contrary to the whole purpose of playing to determine a winner and cannot be simply contained; if the game is to flourish and engage public confidence, cheating must be clearly condemned with an eye to expunging it (pp. 72-73).

This is an eloquent explanation of a wise ruling that effected extraordinary justice.

A Thought Experiment: Heroic Justice or Ghastly Inhumanity?

Thought experiments are used in philosophy and other disciplines to investigate the nature of something by constructing a theoretical situation. Often an impossibility in real life, the situation is nevertheless useful for considering and discussing a concept. The following thought experiment concerns justice and is preceded by two actual news events.

First Actual Event

The donor of the first double-hand transplant in Boston last fall has been identified. Forty-year-old Steven Lloyd of New Hampshire died last October after sudden bleeding in his brain. His wife Judi told WCVB-TV she decided to donate many of his organs.

"Even though he and I didn't discuss it, I knew that he would be fine about it because he helped everybody. I made the decision to donate the rest of his organs, why not donate his hands?"

The hands went to Richard Mangino of Revere (WCVB-TV, 08/21/2014).

<u>Second Actual Event</u>

In 1978 Lawrence Singleton abducted, raped, and mutilated 16 year-old Mary Vincent, severing her arms below the elbows with an ax. Singleton was sentenced to 14 years in prison and was paroled after serving eight years. In 1997 he was convicted of another murder and sentenced to execution. He died of cancer in 2001 in a Florida prison.

<u>Thought Experiment: Judge Brown's Ruling</u>

In the fall of 2010 Richard McDaniel abducted Brenda Robinson and raped her. Following the rape, McDaniel severed both of Robinson's hands with a hatchet, approximately two inches above her wrists. McDaniel was apprehended and convicted of kidnapping, rape, and acting with depraved indifference to human life. He confessed to all charges after Robinson's positive identification of him in a police suspect lineup.

At trial the jury did not find in favor of McDaniel's plea of *not guilty by reason of mental defect*. His attorney, Carlton Graham, argued the repulsiveness of the crime was sufficient to prove McDaniel's insanity. As a previously twice convicted violent felon, McDaniel could have been sentenced to life imprisonment without the possibility of parole. However, prior to sentencing, presiding Judge Mason T. Brown read a magazine story describing a recent, successful double-hand transplant accomplished at Brigham and Women's Hospital in Boston. (One of over three-hundred such successful procedures in the United States.)

Judge Brown stunned the court when he sentenced McDaniel to amputation of both hands for donation to the United Network for Organ Sharing (UNOS). In exchange for his donation, Brenda Robinson will receive two suitable, matching hands from the organ sharing bank. Acting within his discretion, Brown ruled if Robinson refused the transplant McDaniel still would be sentenced to life imprisonment without the possibility of parole.

A spokesperson for the American Civil Liberties Union, citing its policy against harsh sentences that "stand in the way of a just and equal society" and the Eighth Amendment's prohibition of "cruel and unusual punishment," plan an appeal to have Judge Brown's ruling set aside (ACLU, 2015).

Note: To constitute depraved indifference, the defendant's conduct must be so morally deficient and so lacking in regard for a human life that he or she warrants the same criminal liability as a person who intentionally causes a death. Depraved indifference focuses on the risk created by the defendant's conduct rather than the injuries actually resulting.

Questions for Consideration

1. Does Judge Brown's sentence constitute "cruel and unusual" (i.e. inhumane) punishment? If so, why? Do you believe it is likely the ACLU would prevail in its appeal of this sentence? If so, why?

2. Does Judge Brown's sentence go beyond *talion law* (aka "eye-for-eye" justice)?

3. What is your *feeling* about this sentence? (You are *not* being asked, "What are your thoughts?")

4. Do you believe this sentence is an instance of heroic justice or ghastly inhumanity?

5. John Milton wrote of "justice tempered with mercy." Does this sentence violate Milton's principle?

V. Heroism as Wisdom

The older I grow the more I distrust the familiar doctrine that age brings wisdom.

H.L. Mencken

Wisdom doesn't necessarily come with age, sometimes age just shows up all by itself.

Tom Wilson

William James characterized wisdom as knowing what to overlook. Samuel Coleridge spoke of it as common sense in an uncommon degree. Aesop communicated it through fables. Five books of the Old Testament are devoted to it (Job, Psalms, Proverbs, Ecclesiastes, and the Song of Solomon). And the word philosophy is derived from the Greek words for love (*phileo*) and wisdom (*sophos*).

Wisdom is not synonymous with intelligence, which is the ability to acquire and understand information and utilize it in problem solving. Jesus made this point when he told the story commonly referred to as "The Parable of the Rich Fool:

And he told them this parable: "The ground of a certain rich man produced a good crop. He thought to himself, 'What shall I do? I have no place to store my crops.'

"Then he said, 'This is what I'll do. I will tear down my barns and build bigger ones, and there I will store all my grain and my goods. And I'll say to myself, "You have plenty of good things laid up for many years. Take life easy; eat, drink and be merry." '

"But God said to him, 'You fool! This very night your life will be demanded from you. Then who will get what you have prepared for yourself?'

"This is how it will be with anyone who stores up things for himself but is not rich toward God" (Luke 12: 16-21, New International Version).

The phrase "rich fool" might seem an oxymoron. At the least it is counterintuitive to think of a rich man as a fool. The parable is the story of an intelligent businessman who was foolish to presume that he had many years of life remaining. Jesus introduced this parable with the admonishment that "a man's life does not consist in the abundance of his possessions" (Luke 12: 15, New International Version).

A real-life example of an intelligent but unwise man is Dr. Scott Peck, arguably America's best known psychiatrist in the 1980's. Referred to in chapter III, his bestseller, *The Road Less Traveled*, sold over six million copies, was translated into 20 languages, and is the longest running book ever on the *New York Times* bestsellers list. There is no disputing this Harvard Medical School graduate's intelligence or giftedness as a writer. Nevertheless, in spite of the excellent advice he dispensed to millions of people, Peck admitted to significant failures in managing his own life. Concerning his alcohol dependency he wrote,

> I am strongly habituated to alcohol. I eagerly look forward to my gin in quite heavy doses at the end of the day. This habit has become more entrenched over the years. I dearly love the solace it brings me - the relaxation from having the edge taken off my consciousness - and I tend to adjust my day around the "cocktail hour" - or two or three hours (1995, p. 43).

About his smoking he wrote,

Without nicotine for a couple of waking hours I become sick. For over forty years now I have used smoking, somewhat like alcohol, to provide me with brief respites from concentration and rewards for periods of hard mental work. No work requires such intense concentration as writing, and if I ever kick this fierce addiction it will probably only be at a time when I have ceased to write anymore (pp. 42-43).

And regarding his serial adultery he wrote,

My sexual infidelity is a glaring example of the unreasonableness of romance. I would never have been diagnosed as a full-blown "sex addict," but in some ways it was surely a compulsion. A purely rational human being would have known better. I, however, am not purely rational, and this irrational part of me had to have its due. I might not have survived otherwise, but I always wished I could have been a different kind of person who did not need such an outlet. ... Extramarital sex is ... a new body and a new person to be explored. A new territory. It is also forbidden territory, and for some that might be a turn-on. For me it never was. Whatever my psychology, the pure newness of another woman was my primary aphrodisiac (pp. 28-30).

Wisdom is a character trait; its synonyms include insight, judgment, discernment, perceptiveness, and sagacity. It is integral to life management if overall contentment with life is the desired goal. Wisdom is related to morality in that right conduct is necessary for life satisfaction. Biblical scholar Luke Timothy Johnson expressed the importance of wisdom when he addressed the purpose of philosophy:

Classical Greek philosophers Socrates, Aristotle, and Plato are fine - if thinking is what you want. But the word philosophy means "love of wisdom," not "love of thinking." What about solid advice about how to be a good father or friend; or how to grow old gracefully; or know what true happiness is? Where can you find philosophy that tells you not how to think well, but how to live well? (2007, p. 40).

Peck's authorized biography describes his life as a life mismanaged. His wife divorced him late in life and his relationships with his children were either strained or nonexistent. His biographer, Arthur Jones, observed,

Peck was indeed deeply regretting his extremely troubled relationships with his three children. Perversely, he couldn't, or wouldn't, admit the extent to which he was responsible for the fissures and faults that had caused the breech. An unparalleled wordsmith in conversation, he was unable or unwilling to express remorse sufficient to the damage done, in words that sincerely conveyed what he felt. Or ought to have felt (2007, p. 268).

Concerning his father, Christopher Peck surmised that his father was not a Jekyll and Hyde character,

... because Jekyll split himself into vice and virtue, but Scotty's virtue was really a sham. His narcissism left him a very lonely person, and his saintliness (which I found creepier than his cruelty) was a plea for love. I don't think he loved because he enjoyed loving others; he loved in order to be loved back (p. 274).

Among other accomplishments, Ludwig Wittgenstein is well-known for his observation that the purpose of philosophy is "to show the fly the way out of the fly bottle" (1991, p. 87). He believed philosophers had a long history of using esoteric language to address meaningless questions, leaving readers to fly around inside a bottle in a futile effort at escape. Wittgenstein would have found the philosophy of Viktor Frankl agreeable. (Wittgenstein died in 1951, eight years before the publication of Frankl's memoir, *Man's Search for Meaning*.) A psychiatrist and Holocaust survivor, Frankl's philosophy is practical and expressed in unambiguous language. *Man's Search for Meaning* is regarded as a classic in both psychotherapy and philosophy. Written in nine successive days shortly after regaining his freedom, it has been translated into 24 languages and sold over ten million copies. In the preface Frankl explains the purpose of his writing: "I wanted simply to convey to the reader by way of concrete example that life holds a potential meaning under any conditions, even the most miserable ones" (2006, p. xiv).

Like Peck, Frankl was a brilliant psychiatrist who wrote a bestselling book. Unlike Peck, Frankl's personal life is exemplary of heroic wisdom. The school of psychotherapy associated with him, *logotherapy* (also known as *existential therapy*), teaches the philosophical approach to life he not only advocated, but lived:

> Let me explain why I have employed the term "logotherapy" as the name for my theory. Logos is a Greek word which denotes "meaning." Logotherapy, or, as it has been called by some authors, "The Third Viennese School of Psychotherapy," focuses on the meaning of human existence as well as on man's search for such a meaning. According to logotherapy, this striving to find a meaning in one's life is the primary motivational force in man. That is why I speak

of a *will to meaning* in contrast to the pleasure principle (or, as we could also term it, the *will to pleasure*) on which Freudian psychoanalysis is centered, as well as in contrast to the will to power on which Adlerian psychology, using the term "striving for superiority," is focused (2006, pp. 98-99).

Frankl agreed with the analysis of Albert Camus, who believed, "There is but one truly serious philosophical problem, and that is suicide. Judging whether life is or is not worth living amounts to answering the fundamental question of philosophy" (1955, p. 3). Camus was not encouraging suicide but using it as a foil to make the point that when a person chooses to live, which most people do, it becomes that person's responsibility to determine how to live in order to have a meaningful life. Implicit in Camus' analysis is anyone who does not commit suicide is admitting to the possibility of a meaningful life, even under the most miserable of conditions.

The most miserable of conditions began for Frankl in 1944 when he was transported to the concentration camp at Auschwitz, where he survived as a slave laborer. He could have avoided this by emigrating to England, as did Freud. But this would have meant abandoning his parents, so he opted to remain in Vienna.

The wisdom of Frankl is no more apparent than in his teaching of *tragic optimism*. He believed there are three unavoidable tragedies in life: pain, guilt, and death. Moreover, each person is challenged to bring meaning to these inevitable misfortunes. He suggested using pain to direct achievement; using guilt to become a better person; and using death as an incentive to manage time expeditiously. Explaining why he chose the word "optimism" as part of the description for this approach to life he wrote:

... what matters is to make the best of any given situation. "The best," however, is that which in Latin is called *optimum* - hence the reason I speak of tragic optimism, that is, an optimism in the face of tragedy and in view of the human potential which at its best always allows for: (1) turning suffering into a human achievement and accomplishment; (2) deriving from guilt the opportunity to change oneself for the better; and (3) deriving from life's transitoriness an incentive to take responsible action (2006, pp. 137-138).

Fankl's life has been chronicled by his grandson, Alex Vesely, in the documentary "Viktor and I" (2011). Using stories told by Frankl's family and closest colleagues, the essence of one of the great thinkers of the 20th century is brought into focus. Vesely's tribute to his grandfather shows Frankl as he was seen by students, peers, friends, relatives, and acquaintances, both professional and private. There is no mistaking his wisdom, which he generously shared with others through books, lectures, interviews, and personal encounters. Moreover, there is no mistaking the consistency between what he taught and how he lived.

The foreword to the 2006 edition of *Man's Search for Meaning* was written by Rabbi Harold Kushner, an accomplished writer in his own right. There he wrote:

... we give our suffering meaning by the way in which we respond to it. ...Frankl's most enduring insight, one that I have called on in my own life and in countless counseling situations (is): Forces beyond your control can take away everything you possess except one thing, your freedom to choose how you will respond to the situation. You cannot control what happens to you in life, but you can always control what you feel and what you do about what happens to you (Frankl, 2006, p. x).

With these words Kushner encapsulates logotherapy and expresses his appreciation for a principle taught by Frankl and by which he lived.

VI. Heroism as Integrity

Joe Louis is a credit to his race, the human race.

Jimmy Cannon

Integrity is the quality of being of sound moral principle. People with integrity are honest, sincere, and honorable. Fred Rogers ("Mister Rogers") addressed integrity when speaking at the 1992 Boston University commencement: "Always behave in such a way that you'll never be ashamed of the truth about yourself" (1992). Boxing legend Joe Louis never had to be ashamed of the truth about himself. He showed himself as a man of integrity in his toughest fight, the one he had with the Internal Revenue Service.

In a locker room after his fight with Rocky Marciano a doctor carefully studied Louis' swollen and lumpy face.

"Joe, you can't fight for at least three months," said Dr. Vincent Nardiello as he shone his small flashlight into the fighter's eyes. "Doc," Louis responded, "Do you mind if I don't fight any more at all?" (McRae, 2002, p. 279).

On the morning of October 26, 1951 Jimmy Cannon described middle-aged, battle-worn Joe Louis:

> He is an honorable man of simple dignity who works at the dirtiest of all games with a crude nobility. As a pugilist this is a guy whose deportment matches his skills. Even now, at thirty-seven, slow and often clumsy, Louis is a reliable performer. The errors he makes are caused by a disobedient body. But his gameness is unimpaired and his intentions are pure (1951).

Cannon's sentimentality for the man who was the heavyweight champion of the world for 11 years came from memories like the one in 1948 after the first Joe Wolcott fight. Although Louis won, "His face was swollen. He looked like a loser" (McRae, 2002, p. 275). Before Cannon could ask his first post-fight interview question, Louis remembered that Cannon had not been feeling well and asked him, "How's your cold?" (p. 275).

Three years later Louis stepped into the ring to face Rocky Marciano in a non-title fight. Louis had retired in 1949, leaving the title to be claimed first by Ezzard Charles and then Joe Wolcott. Marciano was a rising star who would eventually wrest the heavyweight championship from Wolcott. Well aware his best days were behind him, Louis came out of retirement in 1950 intending to earn enough money to settle a $500,000 tax debt owed to the Internal Revenue Service.

Generosity, patriotism, reckless spending, and misplaced trust combined to erode the fortune he had accumulated over a seventeen-year career.

> When he earned over $371,000 in his first two years as a professional boxer, Louis immediately helped family and friends all over the country. For example, he voluntarily paid back to the government welfare payments his stepfather had received during the Great Depression… one month after the bombing of Pearl Harbor, the generous Louis gave his entire $65,200 fee (about $700,000 in today's money) from a fight to the Naval Relief Fund. Less than three months later, he gave his $45,882 purse from another fight (about $500,000 today) to the Army Relief Fund. Ever the Patriot, he halted his lucrative boxing career and enlisted as a private, earning only $21 a month (Folsom, 1997).

Ironically, the total of Louis' donations to the war effort ($111,082) was nearly equal to his original tax debt ($117,000). Unfortunately, by the time the I.R.S. made him aware of his debt the interest on it increased it to over a million dollars. In addition to the original debt he was being taxed on the money he was earning in his effort to pay off the debt. Reflecting on this Sisyphean task, he said "When you owe that kind of money you can't get out...it's like doing roadwork on a treadmill. The faster you run, the faster they move that treadmill against you" (McRae, 2002, p. 288).

It's unfortunate that of the innumerable photographs of Joe Louis the one most famous is from the Marciano fight and the least indicative of Louis' greatness. It shows him dazed and flat of his back, his body draped over the ring's bottom rope. Marciano felt so bad about the beating he gave his boyhood idol that Rocky cried and apologized to Louis after the fight. The ex-champion thanked the future champion for agreeing to the match and an opportunity for a payday. Louis earned $135,000 that night, most of which he turned over to the I.R.S.

Regrettable is the Marciano fight was not the Brown Bomber's final humiliation. Although it was his last boxing match, it was not the last time he entered the ring. Desperate for money, in 1956 he turned to professional wrestling. Balding and paunchy, Louis was as embarrassed by his aging body as by the pseudo-athletic farce in which he was participating. Before his quixotic effort to settle with the I.R.S. was over, he would further lower himself by appearing on television game shows. Even when he and his wife, Rose, managed to win $60,000 on the show *High Finance*, his $30,000 share went to the I.R.S. As if to prove that humiliation knows no depth, the champion traveled with a circus as a make-believe lion tamer. Armed with a whip, he feigned mastery over a lion who, like Louis, had grown old and devitalized.

It has been said the members of the United States Congress would vote to exempt themselves from the law of gravity if they could. Yet, Congress showed no regard for Louis' wartime generosity when they voted to reject a bill proposed by Alfred Sieminski (Democrat, New Jersey) to forgive Louis' tax debt. Those who voted "no" on that proposal were quite unlike the man of whom sportswriter Milton Gross wrote: "He was a symbol of integrity. He was a man of unimpeachable pride and steadfast principle" (McCrea, 2002, p. 297).

VII. Heroism as Perseverance

Perseverance is the hard work you do after you get tired of the hard work you already did.

Newt Gingrinch

Perseverance is persistence in pursuing a goal or course of action often in spite of difficulties, obstacles, or discouragement. Elyn Saks knows what it means to persevere. In spite of living with schizophrenia since she was eight-years-old, she graduated from Vanderbilt University (valedictorian), Oxford University, Yale Law School, and earned a Ph.D. in psychoanalytic science. A cancer survivor, she is an Associate Dean of the University of California Law School, a recognized expert in mental health law, and the recipient of a MacArthur Foundation "genius award." Concerning her life with schizophrenia she has written,

> My life today is not without its troubles. I have a major mental illness. I will never fully recover from schizophrenia. I will always need to be on antipsychotic medication and in talk therapy. I will always have good days and bad, and I still get sick. ...
> My psychosis is a waking nightmare, in which my demons are so terrifying that all my angels have already fled. ...
> That said, I don't wish to be seen as regretting that I missed the life I could have had if I'd not been ill. Nor am I asking anyone for pity. What I rather wish to say is that the humanity we all share is more important than the mental illness we may not (2007, pp. 334, 336).

Theodore Giesel, better known by his pen name, Dr. Seuss, also knows something of perseverance. His first book, *And to Think I Saw It on Mulberry Street* (1957), was rejected 27 times before it was finally published. Lucy Maude Montgomery, author of *Anne of Green Gables* (2015), and Rabbi Harold Kushner, author of *When Bad Things Happen to Good People* (1981), also received numerous rejection letters before their books were published. These three books are now classics.

Daniel Eugene Reuttiger, immortalized by the movie "Rudy," was an unrecruited, non-scholarship ("walk-on") football player who achieved his goal of playing for the University of Notre Dame (2000). His determination compensated for mediocre athletic and academic abilities. To fulfill his childhood dream "Rudy" had to disregard the unanimous opinion of family and friends that he was pursuing the impossible.

Another highly motivated, minimally skilled athlete is Rocky Balboa, who captured professional boxing's most coveted title: heavyweight champion of the world. However, since Rocky is fictional, the movie bearing his name might not be a reliable source of inspiration (1976). But James Braddock is real and his ascendancy to the heavyweight title is accurately recounted in the movie, "The Cinderella Man" (2005). In 1935 he went from relying on public assistance for supporting his family to being the heavyweight champion of the world.

The documentary "King Gimp" (2012) chronicles the life of Dan Keplinger, an accomplished artist with cerebral palsy so severe that he continuously experiences muscle spasms in one or another part of his body. When majoring in art at Towson State University in Maryland one of the art professors refused to work with him, believing it would be impossible for Keplinger to accomplish all the projects required of art majors. Keplinger believes, "Obstacles and challenges are a part of the human condition. We all face them in everyday life, however we also have a choice as to how to deal with them." (Leibs, 2009).

David Hartman, M.D. persevered in pursuit of his dream of being a physician. After receiving letters of rejection from nine medical schools he was accepted by Temple University and became the first blind person to earn a medical degree. A psychiatrist, his remarkable, inspiring story is told in *White Cane, White Coat: The Extraordinary Oddysey of a Blind Physician* (1978).

These examples of perseverance notwithstanding, there are instances when the pursuit of a dream should come to an end. In this vein Augusten Burroughs, a witty and insightful contemporary writer, offers this advice: "If you spend 20 years chasing something, is it admirable to keep trying? Or did you pass admirable several miles back, and it's getting closer to straightjacket time?" (2016, p. 96). Another perceptive author, Judith Viorst, has written:

> ...the road to human development is paved with renunciation. Throughout our life we grow by giving up. We give up some of our deepest attachments to others. We give up certain cherished parts of ourselves. We must confront, in the dreams we dream, as well as in our intimate relationships, all that we never will have and never will be. Passionate investment leaves us vulnerable to loss. And sometimes, no matter how clever we are, we must lose (1986, p. 16).

The encouraging adage, "What would you do if you did not have to worry about failure?" speaks to pursuing a dream without any instruction as to when to abandon that dream. No doubt there are dreams that would have come true had they not been forsaken. Nevertheless, some dreams should be relinquished. The challenge is knowing when to discontinue the chase. The problem with commending people who wisely gave up on a dream is they remain relatively unknown. Movies and memoirs are not produced telling the stories of those who gave up the life they dreamed of in order to have the life that was waiting for them. John Greenlief Whittier opined, "For all sad words of tongue or pen. The saddest are these: 'It might have been!'" (1897). If there exists an alternate universe that includes things that "might have been," there is no human access to it. Still, those who have lived these words of Walt Whitman are to be admired: "From this hour I ordain myself loos'd of limits and imaginary lines" (2017).

VIII.   Heroism as Resilience

You learn a few things as you go along and one of them is that the world breaks everyone and afterward many are strong in the broken places. Those that it does not break it kills. It kills the very good and the very gentle and the very brave impartially. If you are none of these you can be sure it will kill you too but there will be no special hurry.

Ernest Hemingway, *A Farewell to Arms*

Resilience is the ability to recover from misfortune; to return to a previous condition or level of functionality. Michelle Fox not only exemplifies resilience, she epitomizes it. In February of 2009 she was feeding her three-year-old daughter when her ex-husband accidentally discharged a shotgun in the left side of her face. Her losses were catastrophic. She not only lost her eyes, but her face was so disfigured that attempts at facial reconstructive surgery failed. Now she,

> ... wears a prosthetic face made of silicone and acrylic that covers the width of her face from her eyebrows to her upper lip. It includes artificial blue eyes and lashes. She has forgiven her ex-husband ... (and) she has found new love. She has tried snowboarding, ran a 5k, and is an avid cook who prepares meals from scratch without help (McMahon, 2014).

Unfathomably, Michelle reports, "I'm happier now than before my accident. I never thought I would say that when I first became blind. I was feeling like I was all alone in a big black room. I'd cry and cry. Now it doesn't matter" (2014). She attributes her resilience to her revitalized relationship with

God, a new romance, supportive friends, and Reiki, a form of alternative medicine.

Albert Camus wrote: "In the midst of winter, I finally learned there is within me an invincible summer. ... There is thus a will to live without rejecting anything of life, which is the virtue I honor most in this world" (1952). One of Michelle's last memories after the accident was being airlifted to the hospital. She was asked by the pilot if she wanted to live. Unable to speak, she nodded as hard as she could. Eight years later, every day Michelle Fox attaches her prosthetic face and gets on with her day - an unusual practice that's part of an extraordinary life.

Perhaps the most frequently quoted of Friedrich Nietzsche's aphorisms is, "That which does not kill me makes me stronger" (1997, p. 6). Bob Shumaker personifies this adage. He endured starvation and torture as a prisoner of war for eight years in North Vietnam, including three years in solitary confinement. Yet, when asked if he would have preferred a life without the POW experience, he responded, "no." Not minimizing the agony of those years, Shumaker said, "I learned things about myself I could not have learned otherwise" (2010).

Shumaker is not as well-known as Paul Wittgenstein, who resumed his career as a concert pianist *after* having his right arm amputated during World War I or Ludwig von Beethovan, who wrote his Ninth Symphony when he was virtually deaf. Famous or not, along with Michelle Fox, all of them are real-life demonstrations of heroic resilience.

Reframing

Although *framing* is not a formal psychological term, it is an essential concept in the practice of psychotherapy. It refers to how people describe their situations and largely determines how they feel about their circumstances. A character in David

Taylor's *The Myth of Certainty* alludes to framing when she says, "You have everything you need for your contentment or misery within the confines of your own heart" (1986, p. 142). Resilience almost always requires *reframing*, specifically, shifting attention away from losses and toward things retained. Richard Cohen is a nationally syndicated political columnist and four time Pulitzer Prize recipient. In addition, he is nearly blind, twice a cancer survivor, and limited by multiple sclerosis. In his memoir, *Blindsided: Living a Life Above Illness - A Reluctant Memoir*, he shares a daily conversation he has with himself, lest he despair owing to his continually deteriorating body:

> I feel weak because I acknowledge the realities of my life. We exist in a culture that celebrates strength. men are strong and self-reliant. I am weakened and need the help of others. There is no escape from the rust I see on my body.
>
> I must rise above the culture of perfection and remember that I can be even if I cannot *do*. I am learning to acknowledge weakness, accept assistance, and discover new forms of self-definition. My formula has changed. I do not read self-absorbed men's magazines or go to Vin Diesel movies. A new male idea will have to do. I cannot allow myself to be held captive by old dreams.
>
> Success comes today by a different standard, measured by more cerebral achievements and often centered on the lives of my children. ...Dealing with challenges to health is a great ally in nurturing that change in priorities (2004, p. 22).

Like Richard Cohen, Travis Roy has met the challenge of reframing his life. A spinal cord injury 11 seconds into his first college hockey game left him a quadriplegic. In his memoir, *Eleven Seconds: A Story of Tragedy, Courage, and Triumph*, he wrote:

> Still, when I think about my life, I feel lucky. No, I can't do the physical things I used to be able to do, but I can laugh and cry and enjoy the people around me. I've found these are the most important things in life. ... I can still set goals and find ways to achieve them. I've learned that when life takes an unexpected turn, we have to hang onto the goals that are still realistic and reassess those that are not. ... Setting new goals, finding new passions - these are the things that prevent us becoming stagnant. They can lead us to accomplishments of which we only once dreamed (1998, p. 236).

Reframing sometimes takes the form of focusing on reasons to live rather than reasons to die. Gordon Livingston, a psychiatrist, employs this strategy with suicidal patients:

> When confronted with a suicidal person I seldom try to talk them out of it. Instead I ask them to examine what it is that has so far dissuaded them from killing themselves. Usually this involves finding out what the connections are that tether that person to life in the face of nearly unbearable psychic pain. ...Suicide is the ultimate expression of preoccupation with self. Instead of just expressing the sympathy and fear that suicidal people evoke in those around them, therapists included, I think it is reasonable to confront them with the selfishness and anger implied in any act of self-destruction.
> Does this approach work to prevent someone from killing himself?

Sometimes. In thirty-three years of practicing psychiatry I have lost this argument only once (2004, p. 72).

Livingston redirects his patients' attention to the reason or reasons they have for living since that is what has sustained them to the present. He also turns their attention away from themselves and toward those who will be affected, if not devastated, by their suicide.

Hedonic Adaptation

Hedonic adaptation is the psychological process by which people become accustomed to a positive or negative event or situation such that the emotional effects are attenuated over time. Long before hedonic adaptation became a part of psychological jargon, Fyodor Dostoevsky wrote, "Man is a pliant animal, a being who gets accustomed to anything" (2017). Hedonic adaptation contributes to resilience, enabling people like Michelle Fox, Richard Cohen, and Travis Roy to become accustomed to their circumstances and devote their time and attention to making the most of the life they have rather than lamenting the life they lost.

Charles Krauthammer is well-known as a syndicated political columnist and frequent commentator on television. Barely noticeable when he appears on television is that he is in a wheelchair, the result of a diving accident when he was a first year medical student at Harvard. Almost immediately after receiving the diagnosis of his catastrophic spinal cord injury he showed resilience:

> Toward the end of my freshman year I was paralyzed in a serious accident. (The) associate dean of students came to see me in intensive care. He asked what he could do for me. I told him that, to keep disaster from

turning into ruin, I had decided to stay in school and with my class (2013, p. 35).

Krauthammer graduated with his class, completed a residency in psychiatry, and accomplished board certification in psychiatry and neurology. After a brief, productive career as a physician he made a career change and became a political analyst. A Pulitzer Prize recipient, his bestselling collection of columns, *Things that Matter: Three Decades of Passions, Pastimes, and Politics* (2013), includes only a single reference to his paralysis, and that as part of a tribute to one of his medical school professors. Krauthammer has adapted to the inconveniences of life in a wheelchair and pursued two demanding careers in addition to meeting responsibilities as a husband and father.

Francesco Clark also dove into a swimming pool and suffered a spinal cord injury. A quadriplegic since age 22, in addition to losing the use of his arms and legs, he lost the ability to perspire, causing an extremely irritating skin condition. Without formal training in either chemistry or dermatology, he developed a lotion to treat his condition. Eventually, this led to the founding of Clark's Botanicals, an international producer and distributor of cosmetic products. Like Krauthammer, almost immediately after the accident and the realization that his life would not be the one he had planned, he prepared for himself for another life. According to Francesco, it is the life to which he has become accustomed (2010).

Conclusion: The Amy Mullins Thought Experiment

Herman Hesse believed the most difficult road for a man to travel is the one that leads him to himself. The man in the following story seems to be traveling this road. Although this encounter is fictional, the woman, Aimee Mullins, is not. All of the information concerning her is factual.

Imagine a man sitting at a bar, taking his last sip of Chardonnay before leaving when a stunning woman takes the seat next to him. Without staring, he sizes her up as late-twenties, impeccably dressed with shoulder-length, perfectly coiffed blond hair, a flawless complexion more like porcelain than skin, and mesmerizing blue eyes. Knowing he'll regret not even trying, he begins a conversation and is delighted by her friendliness. More than that, as if more was necessary to rivet his attention, he finds her pleasantly articulate. Over the next hour, from a series of questions designed to keep the conversation going, he learns she's a Georgetown University graduate where she competed in track-and-field and currently working as an actress and model when not involved in several not-for-profit organizations.

She glances at her watch (fortunately for the first time) and says, "I have an early flight to catch in the morning, I better be going." In synchrony, they rise, extend right hands, and say "Nice to meet you." Emboldened by this serendipitous choreography, he asks for her phone number. As though she expected the question - of course she did, she gets it all the time - she gives him her card, instructing him to use the cell number when he calls.

She leaves without looking back but his eyes never leave her. Returning home with an excitement that precludes falling asleep, he fires up his PC, ostensibly to check for e-mails. Almost immediately he switches to *Google* and types the name, "Aimee Mullins." In less than a second, the first wave of over 500,000 results appears. After ten minutes of reading he has learned much: She attended Georgetown on a full academic scholarship, one of three awarded by the Department of Defense, graduating with honors from the School of Foreign Service. At seventeen she was the youngest person ever to hold top-security clearance at the Pentagon, where she worked summers as an intelligence analyst. In 1999 she made her debut as a runway model in London at the invitation of Alexander McQueen, an internationally renowned fashion designer. She's appeared in *Vogue*, *Harper's Bazaar*, and *Elle.* In addition, she was in *Esquire's* "Women We Love" issue, *People Magazine* as one of the "50 Most Beautiful People," and on *Rolling Stone's* "Annual Hot List." Aimee also had the starring role in a highly acclaimed film, "Cremaster 3."

She mentioned she's an athlete, an understatement. She's featured in exhibits in the NCAA Hall of Fame and Track and Field Hall of Fame and acclaimed in *Sports Illustrated* as one of the "Coolest Women in Sport." At this point he's hardly surprised when reading that the Women's Museum in Dallas, Texas honored her as one of the "Greatest Women of the 20th Century" for her achievements in sports.

The surprise came when he learned that Aimee Mullins is a double amputee! Born without shinbones, both her legs were amputated below the knee when she was a year-old. Her parents decided life with prosthetics would provide her with more mobility than life in a wheelchair. She was born with *fibular hemimelia*, a congenital condition in which large bones in the extremities are absent - a condition that usually occurs in one limb and more often among boys.

More accurately, his reaction was one of shock, not surprise. He had never heard of this condition and there was nothing in Aimee's gait that suggested even an ankle sprain, let alone prosthetic legs under her Cynthia Vincent full-length skirt. A cascade of questions followed: Am I still going to call her? If not, why? Why should "no legs" make a difference? Doesn't this make her all the more impressive? If I do call, how do I bring up what I've learned? ("Oh, I looked you up in *Wikipedia* and learned you're from Allentown, Pennsylvania and that you don't have legs - I mean, real ones.") If I don't call, she'll know why. How can I hurt her by not calling?

He then realized this is about him, not her. He wondered, "Is it that I don't want to hurt her or that I don't want to generate evidence of my shallowness? And if I do call, would it be to reassure myself that I'm not superficial? After all, she gave me her number, I'm the one wrestling with how to proceed."

More self-examination followed: "Why do I need to date a perfect woman? Isn't that what I thought she was until I learned about her disability? How can I even think of her as disabled? Would she be more accomplished if she had legs? And, what if she had legs but was vain and narcissistic with nothing in her biography but a long history of suitors? Would that make her more desirable?"

Postscript

The preceding thought experiment raises several questions concerning the relative value of human characteristics. What are the qualities that make a person worthy of admiration and acclaim? Does Aimee have these qualities? Should her so-called disability discourage a prospective suitor? If so, why? The sardonic adage "Heroes are not born, they are cornered," implies acts of extraordinary heroism result from situations in which there is no choice but to act heroically. Aimee Mullins did not choose to be born with *fibular hemimelia*, neither did she make the decision for a double amputation. However, throughout her life, she has repeatedly chosen to pursue her interests and test her limits. Is she heroic? Another adage teaches, "Determinism is the hand we've been dealt, free will is the choice of how that hand is played." Aimee Mullins has chosen to play her hand by living life to the fullest, challenging and inspiring others to do the same. Is she heroic? Her resiliency is reminiscent of Dax Cowart, who in 1973 was severely burned in an automobile explosion. In the accident he lost two-thirds of his skin, both hands, both eyes, and both ears. He attempted suicide several times and his appeals to have medical treatment discontinued were denied. Eventually, he accepted his lot as "The Man Sentenced to Life," graduated from law school, and married (Wicker, 1989). Like Aimee Mullins, his recovery from misfortune is impressive.

Aimee has said, "The only true disability is a crushed spirit" (Lafave, 2010). Certainly she has displayed resilience in addition to a host of other favorable qualities: confidence, compassion, determination, intelligence, and self-discipline. She also has a sense of humor: "Interesting, from an identity standpoint, what does it mean to have a disability? Pamela Anderson has more prosthetics in her body than I do and nobody calls her disabled" (Mullins, 2009). In this age of cosmetic procedures, it is reasonable to ask why artificial legs would be considered unattractive. No doubt, for some men Aimee's admirable traits would not offset what she's lacking below the knee. For others, her prosthetics would be a non-issue. Apparently the English actor Rupert Friend is in the latter category, he and Aimee were married in 2016.

IX. Heroism as Commitment and Sacrifice

Greater love has no one than this, that he lay down his life for his friends.

John 15:13 (NIV)

There's an old saw about the difference between a hen and pig concerning a bacon and eggs breakfast. The hen makes a contribution; the pig is committed. Commitments are measured by the sacrifices made to keep them. A story told by Kay Jamison, referred to in chapter I, is her recollection of a jet pilot whose commitment to duty cost him his life.

I was standing with my head back, one pigtail caught between my teeth, listening to the jet overhead. The noise was loud, unusually so, which meant that it was close. My elementary school was near Andrews Air Force Base, just out-side Washington; many of us were pilots kids, so the sound was a matter of routine.

The noise of the jet became louder, and I saw the other children in my second-grade class suddenly dart their heads upward. The plane was coming in very low, then it streaked past us, scarcely missing the playground. As we stood there clumped together and absolutely terrified, it flew into the trees, exploding directly in front of us. The ferocity of the crash could be felt and heard in the plane's awful impact; it also could be seen in the frightening but terrible lingering loveliness of the flames that followed. Over the next few days it became clear from the release of the young pilot's final message to the control tower before he died, that he knew he could save his own life by bailing out. He also knew, however, that by doing so he risked that his unaccompanied plane would fall onto the playground and kill those of us who were there (1995, pp. 11-13).

Reflecting on the pilot's sacrifice, Jamison has written: "The dead pilot became a hero, transformed into a scorchingly vivid, completely impossible ideal for what was meant by the concept of duty" (p. 13).

The Battle at Bull Run was the first major engagement of the Civil War. Sullivan Ballou, a Union officer from Rhode Island, wrote to his wife on the eve of the battle. In his letter he eloquently expressed his commitment to the cause for which he would be fighting and, possibly, dying:

> I have no misgivings about, or lack of confidence in, the cause in which I am engaged, and my courage does not halt or falter. ... And I am willing - perfectly willing - to lay down all my joys in this life, to help maintain this Government ...
>
> And how hard it is for me to give up and burn to ashes the future years, when, God willing, we might still have lived and loved together, and seen our sons grow up to honorable manhood around us.
>
> Sarah do not mourn me dead, think I am gone and wait for thee, for we shall meet again (Carroll, 1997, p. 111-112).

One week after writing his letter, Sullivan Ballou was one of 481 Union soldiers killed at the First Battle of Battle of Bull Run.

Eric Liddell's commitment and sacrifice is featured in the Academy Award winning film "Chariots of Fire." (It won four awards in 1981, including Best Picture.) The man who once said, "God made me fast and when I run I feel his pleasure," was favored to win the 100 meter sprint at the 1924 Olympic Games refused to run in a qualifying race because it was held on Sunday (2017). As a matter of conscience, Liddell's commitment to his Christian faith required him to sacrifice the opportunity to win a gold medal.

This was not the last time his commitment would require sacrifice. Liddell died in 1945 in a Japanese internment camp while serving as a missionary in Northern China. The British government earlier had urged British nationals to leave China because of Japanese aggression. Langdon Gilkey, an American teaching in China, was imprisoned with Liddell at the same camp. Years later Gilkey wrote admirably of Liddell:

> He was overflowing with good humour and love for life, and with enthusiasm and charm. It is rare indeed that a person has the good fortune to meet a saint, but he came as close to it as anyone I have ever known (1966, p. 192).

Amy Chua is a Yale University Law School professor, author of two award winning books on international relations, and a recognized scholar in political science, economics, and law. Notwithstanding, she is best known for her book on parenting, *Battle Hymn of the Tiger Mother*, a bestseller translated into 30 languages. Often misunderstood as a manual for parenting and an indictment of Western child-rearing practices, it is actually a story of the difficulty of nurturing self-discipline and other virtues in children without losing their love. Her commitment to parenting as a tiger mother required risks and sacrifices she anticipated.

> Chinese parenting is one of the most difficult things I can think of. You have to be hated sometimes by someone you love and hopefully loves you, and there's

just no letting up, no point at which it suddenly becomes easy. Chinese parents - at least if you're trying to do it in America, where all odds are against you - is a never-ending uphill battle, requiring a 24-7 time commitment, resilience, and guile (pp. 161-162).

But also there were risks and sacrifices she did not foresee. Widespread misunderstanding of her book created a global uproar that included death threats, racial slurs, and accusations of child abuse. In addition to narratives describing her expectations for her daughters are descriptions of the sacrifices she made to support them. Moreover, *Battle Hymn of the Tiger Mother* includes a confession:

> This (book) was supposed to be a story of how Chinese parents are better at raising their kids than Western ones. But instead, it's a bitter clash of cultures, a fleeting taste of glory, and how I was humbled by a thirteen-year-old (2011, p. 1).

X. Heroism in Conflicting Obligations

Two roads diverged in a yellow wood,
And sorry I could not travel both
And be one traveler, long I stood
                    Robert Frost, "The Road Not Taken"

Duties are not performed for duty's sake, but because their
neglect would make the man uncomfortable. A man performs
but one duty - the duty of contenting his spirit, the duty of
making himself agreeable to himself.
                                        Mark Twain

The renowned (some would say, notorious) psychiatrist Thomas Szasz posited, "The quality of our life depends largely on concordance or discordance between our desires and our duties" (1973, p. 47). Whenever that which we *ought* to do coincides with that which we *desire* to do, life proceeds without conflict. Whenever there is discord between duty and desire, decision-making is not so easily accomplished. And whenever one obligation is in conflict with another obligation, moral decision-making becomes especially problematic.

A well-known situation of conflicting obligations is found in the New Testament narrative in which Jesus is asked if the Jewish people have an obligation to pay taxes to the Roman Empire. The question was intended as a conundrum in order to discredit Jesus by befuddling him. The Jewish people recognized God as their only king, thereby rejecting Caesar as their ruler. If Jesus advocated nonpayment of taxes, he would have been branded a traitor to Rome. If he encouraged payment of taxes, he would have lost favor in the Jewish community. His answer adequately addressed what seemed to be conflicting obligations:

But Jesus, knowing their evil intent, said, "You hypocrites, why are you trying to trap me?" Show me the coin used for paying the tax." They brought him a denarius, and he asked them, "Whose portrait is this? And whose inscription?"

"Caesar's," they replied.

Then he said, "Give to Caesar's what is Caesar's, and to God what is God's" (Matthew 22:18-21).

According to Jesus, the obligations were not in conflict. Since Rome's requirement was monetary, paying taxes to Caesar would take nothing away from God. Since God's requirement is obedience to the Ten Commandments and 603 other *mitzvah* (laws) found in the Hebrew Bible, adherence to God's law would take nothing away from Caesar. In this instance there only seemed to be a conflict.

However, such is not always the case. Sir Thomas More, Chancellor to King Henry VIII, had to choose between loyalty to his King and obedience to his Pope, Clement VII. When the King determined he would divorce Catherine of Aragon and marry Anne Boleyne, Sir Thomas refused to support Henry's decision and agreed with the Pope's refusal to annul the marriage. This led to More's trial and conviction for treason and execution by decapitation in 1535.

Another instance of a church and state conflict, albeit with less dire consequences, is that of Eric Liddell, referred to in the previous chapter. When he refused to run on the Sabbath he was representing England in the Olympics. His future king, the Prince of Wales, tried to convince him he had a patriotic obligation to participate. Liddell remained steadfast in his conviction while admitting to the difficulty of choosing God over country.

The practice of medicine also provides occasions for conflicting obligations. In 1998 Dr. Jack Kevorkian administered a lethal cocktail (combination of medications) to

Thomas Youk who was suffering from Lou Gehrig's disease and requested physician-assisted suicide. The procedure was performed in Michigan, where physician-assisted suicide was and remains illegal. As a result, Kevorkian was convicted of second degree murder and sentenced to ten to fifteen years imprisonment. He served eight years, was paroled in 2007, and died in 2011 at the age of 83.

As a physician, Kevorkian was confronted with oppositional obligations. When he graduated from the University of Michigan Medical School in 1952 he affirmed the Hippocratic Oath which conferred upon him the obligations to alleviate patient suffering and refrain from administering lethal medications to a patient. In the case of Thomas Youk, Kevorkian opted for euthanasia, convinced it was the only means for alleviating the patient's suffering.

Kevorkian believed there are cases in which the compassionate thing to do is physician-assisted suicide. This would constitute "the most loving act" advocated by Joseph Fletcher, the best-known proponent of situational ethics. Youk had requested this action and provided written and video recorded informed consent, demonstrating his decision was uninfluenced by Kevorkian or anyone else. Further, by addressing Youk as a suffering human being in need of pain relief, Kevorkian placed the patient above the law. Kevorkian acted in a manner consistent with his belief that a hopelessly suffering human being's choice for physician-assisted suicide is morally right even if not legal.

A similar situation confronted Dr. Max Scur in 1939 when he administered a lethal dose of morphine to a suffering, cancer-riddled patient. The patient was Sigmund Freud, who had asked Schur to promise, "when the time comes, you won't let them torment me unnecessarily" (Gay, 1989, pp. 642-643). Like Kevorkian, Schur placed the alleviation of a patient's pain above the Hippocratic prohibition of lethal medications.

Another striking occurrence of conflicting obligations confronted helicopter pilot Hugh Thompson on perhaps the darkest day of the Vietnam War. It was on that day a United States Army company of infantrymen killed between 350 and 500 unarmed, noncombatant villagers, including women, children, and elderly. First, disbelieving what he saw from a low hover over the My Lai hamlet and then appalled by the wanton slaughter he was witnessing, Major Thompson decided to take action to stop the killing. Assigned to protect soldiers on the ground, he landed his helicopter and ordered his machine gunners to turn their weapons on the American troops if they continued killing the unprotected Vietnamese. Thompson is hailed as a hero in sociologist Samuel Oliner's book, *Do Unto Others: Extraordinary Acts of Ordinary People*. There it is written, "The courage of this helicopter pilot and his rescue of innocent Vietnamese civilians at My Lai is a particularly compelling example of an unusual kind of military heroism" (2007, p. 117). Thompson weighed and considered his mission to protect soldiers on the ground against his moral obligation to protect defenseless people and acted in favor of the latter.

Obligations: Origin and Prioritizing

Principles are necessary for prioritizing conflicting obligations. Without guidelines, moral decision-making is left to the feelings of the decision makers. However agreeable or compassionate might be the actions of More, Liddell, Kevorkian, Schur, and Thompson, it would be unwise to affirm a moral action merely because it emanated from the sentiments of the actor. Lieutenant William Calley, referred to in chapter I as an example of a misguided sense of duty, ordered and participated in the killings at My Lai. He *felt* he acted properly that day. At his trial in 1970 he said:

I was ordered to go in there and destroy the enemy. That was my job that day. That was the mission I was given. I did not sit down and think in terms of men, women, and children. They were all classified as the same, and that's the classification that we dealt with over there, just as the enemy. I felt then and I still do that I acted as I was directed, and I carried out the order that I was given and I do not feel wrong in doing so (2015).

Yet, nearly forty years later, speaking to a Kiwanis Club in Georgia, he issued a public apology for his role in the massacre:

There is not a day that goes by that I do not feel remorse for what happened that day in My Lai. I feel remorse for the Vietnamese who were killed, for their families, for the American soldiers involved and their families. I am very sorry. ... If you are asking why I did not stand up to them when I was given the orders, I will have to say that I was a 2nd Lieutenant getting orders from my commander and I followed them— foolishly, I guess (Nix, 2009).

A prerequisite to prioritizing conflicting obligations is establishing the source of the obligations. Without considering the origins of conflicting duties it would be impossible to prioritize them. For Sir Thomas More and Eric Liddell it was a matter of subordinating an earthly obligation to a heavenly responsibility. This principle was declared by the Apostle Peter when he and the other apostles appeared before the Jewish ruling council.

Having brought in the apostles, they made them appear before the Sanhedrin to be questioned by the high priest. "We gave you strict orders not to teach in this name (Jesus)," he said. "Yet you have filled Jerusalem with your teaching and are determined to make us guilty of this man's blood."

Peter and the other apostles replied: "We must obey God rather than men!" (Acts 5:27-29).

For Drs. Kevorkian and Schur it was a matter of preferring the dying wish of a suffering human being over an oath. For Major Thompson it was a matter of saving lives rather than following orders that had become irrelevant to his mission.

Shakespeare wrote, "Thus conscience does make cowards of us all" (*Hamlet*, 3.1.91). And Jean-Paul Sartre wrote, "Man is condemned to be free; because once thrown into the world, he is responsible for everything he does" (1957, p. 23). Navy SEAL Chris Kyle, the most lethal sniper in American military history, reflected on his duty with these words, "Every person I killed I strongly believe that they were bad. When I do go face God there is going to be lots of things I will have to account for, but killing any of those people is not one of them" (2015). Prioritizing obligations, conflicting as well as nonconflicting, requires conscience and a willingness to take responsibility.

Thought Exercise: "The Confession"

Father Garbriel hears the confession of a man whose voice the priest recognizes. He is certain the confessing man is X. The confession is shocking and disturbing. X confesses to having sexually abused his eight-year-old niece, the daughter of his sister.

Father Gabriel appeals to the man to tell his sister what he's done and have her arrange counseling for her daughter. Further, the priest advises X to end all contact with his niece and seek out counseling for himself without disclosing anything specific that would require the counselor to act as a mandated reporter. (As a priest, Father Gabriel is not a mandated reporter and is required to maintain "priest - penitent confidentiality.")

Questions for Consideration

1. In your opinion, does Father Gabriel have a moral obligation beyond the counsel he has given X?

2. Is it justifiable to exempt the clergy from being "mandated reporters" while teachers, physicians, and mental health professionals are not exempt? (Note: Attorneys are not legally required to report suspected or known child abuse, but in some jurisdictions they are permitted to use their discretion.)

3. In a criminal proceeding, a spouse cannot be compelled to testify against a spouse. This would include a case of child abuse. What is the reason for this feature of the law? In your opinion, is it a necessary and important feature?

XI. Heroism as Love for Humanity

It is easier to love humanity as a whole than to love one's neighbor.

Eric Hoffer

When I was young I admired clever people. As I grew old I came to admire kind people.

Abraham Joshua Heschel

In 1948 Albert Camus, an atheist, was invited by the Dominican monks of Latour-Maubourg to address them on the topic: "What Unbelievers Expect from Christians." Sensing honesty in their assurance that they were not seeking to engage him in a debate, he accepted the invitation. As to be expected from an existentialist, he told them he expected Christians to:

> get away from abstraction and confront the blood-stained face history has taken on today. The grouping we need is a grouping of men resolved to speak out clearly and pay up personally (Blackburn, 2011).

In addition, he expected Christians to take action to alleviate human suffering, especially when it cannot be eradicated: "Perhaps we cannot prevent this world from being a world in which children are tortured. But we can reduce the number of tortured children" (2011). This expectation is consistent with the theme of one of his novels, *The Plague* (1948), in which one of the characters, Dr. Rieux, exhaustedly works to combat a plague knowing he is laboring in a lost cause.

Common wisdom teaches *anything to good to be true isn't*, but the same cannot be said about anything *too bad*. When Richard Kuklinski was asked how many murders he committed, "The Ice Man" hesitated before settling on an estimate of 230. This astonishing number and Kuklinski's reflection that he killed without a tinge of emotion mark him as pathologically bad, if not evil. If it is possible to be pathologically bad, is it also possible to be pathologically good? In this chapter Zell Kravinsky, Simone Weil, Albert Lexie, and Albert Schweitzer are presented as examples of extreme benevolent behavior and, if such exists, pathological goodness.

The American Psychiatric Association's *Diagnostic and Statistical Manual* does not have the category *pathological altruism* or anything resembling it. Nevertheless, can altruism be expressed to a degree that it is symptomatic of a psychological disorder rather than an expression of sheer human decency? Perhaps interest in the possibility that extreme kindness indicates a mental illness arises from an internal conflict. On one hand we believe our lives to be our own and are entitled to live for ourselves. Simultaneously, a voice within speaks to us about the needs of others and our obligations to them. That voice informs us the resources we enjoy spending on self-gratification come from grace (unmerited favor) and constitute the test of which Mother Teresa spoke when she posited we are indebted to the poor because they provide us with an opportunity to prove we are as charitable as we claim. In Nick Hornby's novel, *How to Be Good*, a wife finds her husband's extreme kindness so discomforting she contemplates divorcing him (2001).

A century ago William James expressed his conviction that philosophy's great challenge was to refute the assertion of its detractors who claimed since "philosophy bakes no bread" it is a frivolous discipline (1907, p. 83). A century later, Timothy Luke Johnson asserted the purpose of studying philosophy is not to "think well" but to "live well" (2007). And Ludwig Wittgenstein's assertion that "the purpose of philosophy is to show the fly the way out of the fly bottle" is well known (1922). The question of the possibility of pathological goodness is worth addressing because the answer will buttress the conviction of James, Johnson, and Wittgenstein that philosophy's *raison d'etre* is to contribute to living well. The issues of charity and self-sacrifice can generate guilt if the questions of *how much charity* and *how much sacrifice* are left unanswered. Any effort to mitigate guilt and contribute to living well is nearly as practical as baking bread. Out of this conviction the possibility of *pathological goodness* is worthy of consideration.

Zell Kravinsky

Zell Kravinski once sought goodness through prayer. "I used to pray to God to be good. I used to fantasize about a pill that I could take that would make me good. Then I realized it's putting the cart before the horse. First, you do the good deed" (Fagone, 2006). In the wake of his existential epiphany it is indisputable that Kravinsky has sought goodness through charity. He has donated a kidney to a stranger and expressed a willingness to donate the one remaining. "What if someone needed it who could produce more good than me?" (Strom, 2003). Kravinsky believes, "To withhold a kidney from someone who would otherwise die means valuing one's own life at 4,000 times that of a stranger" (Singer, 2006). He arrived at that figure from the survivor ratio of donors who undergo the procedure (4,000 to 1). It cannot be said were he better educated he would not be so philanthropic. He has earned two Ph.D.'s, one in rhetoric and a second in English literature, and nearly accomplished a third in cultural anthropology.

To say Kravinsky is charitable is an understatement. He has donated $45,000,000 to various causes, including the largest donation ever made to the Center for Diseases Control ($6.2 million dollars). It cannot be said that Kravinsky should see a mental health professional. He lives with one, his wife Emily is a psychiatrist. Notwithstanding, a family friend offered this observation of Kravinsky's benevolent actions: "Sometimes there's a slightly pathological element to them" (Singer, 2006). Paul Find, Professor of Psychiatry at Temple University, opined: "If he does (make a second kidney donation) then there's something really wrong. And, if I was his wife, I'd have him committed" (Singer, 2006). And if altruism's vehement critic, Ayn Rand, had known Zell Kravinski, she would have challenged his philosophy, if not his sanity:

> If a man accepts the ethics of altruism, he suffers the following consequences (in proportion to the degree of his acceptance): (1) Lack of self-esteem - since his first concern in the realm of values is not how to live his life, but how to sacrifice it. (2) Lack of respect for others - since he regards mankind as a herd of doomed beggars crying for someone's help (1961, p. 49).

Is Zell Kravinsky pathologically benevolent? The renowned psychiatrist Thomas Szasz, were he alive today, would say *no* from the premise that behaviors cannot be "sick."

> Strictly speaking, disease or illness can only affect the body; hence there can be no mental illness. "Mental illness" is a metaphor. Minds can be "sick" only in the sense that jokes are "sick" or economies are "sick" (1973, p. 267).

In *The Myth of Mental Illness* Dr. Szasz argues when individuals are diagnosed as mentally ill solely on the basis of their behavior the diagnosis cannot be justified. He believed the absence of a standard for human behavior makes it impossible to speak of any behavior as "sick." He did believe a behavior is criminal when it is not in conformity to the law; but he did not believe any illegal behavior constitutes a mental illness:

> Psychiatric expert testimony (is) mendacity masquerading as medicine (1973, p. 40). There can be no humane penology so long as punishment masquerades as "correction." No person or group has the right to correct a human being; only God does (pp. 42-43).

Szasz, who eschewed most psychiatric labels, would be quick to point out mental health professionals do not include *pathological benevolence* or anything approximating it as a psychiatric diagnosis. In contrast, the DSM-5 includes personality disorders that imply an individual's *pathological badness* toward others (antisocial personality disorder, borderline personality disorder, and narcissistic personality disorder).

G.K. Chesterton observed, "Art, like morality, requires drawing a line someplace" (2010, 839). Line drawing also applies to distinguishing normal from abnormal behavior. But who decides where to place this line and how this decision should be made? Why is the altruism of Mother Teresa worthy of a Nobel prize and Zell Kravinski's suggestive of a mental illness? Moreover, to be consistent, his mental health cannot be questioned without also questioning the psychological well-being of Jesus Christ who taught, "Greater love has no one than this, that he lay down his life for his friends" and then proceeded to do exactly that (John 15:13). Kravinsky maintains, "The only cure for the disease of wealth is to spend money" (Singer, 2006). This view is reminiscent of Jesus' instruction to the wealthy man who asked: "Good teacher, what must I do to inherit eternal life" (Luke 18:18)? Jesus responded, "Sell everything you have and give to the poor, and you will have treasure in heaven. Then come follow me" (Luke 18:22). Unlike that rich man, Kravinsky has divested himself of his wealth.

Perhaps the reason why his sacrifices raise a suspicion of some psychological disorder while those of Mother Teresa are deemed worthy of sainthood is the sacrificial calling of Mother Teresa has the endorsement of a religious order and Nobel committee. In contrast, Kravinsky's unique altruism is relatively unknown, having been publicized only in feature stories characterizing his generosity as eccentric, if not bizarre. In addition, perhaps it is his calculated self-destruction that provokes dubiety concerning his mental health.

Kravinsky rationalizes seeking out opportunities for distributing his assets and, if he could have his way, sacrificing his quality of life with a utilitarian argument: "No one should have a second car until everyone has one. And no one should have two kidneys until everyone has one" (Strom, 2003). However, the guiding principle of utilitarianism is not simply *the greatest good for the most number* but *the greatest good for the most number of involved parties*. His charity to unknown others is at the expense of those known to him - his wife and children. This makes his love indiscriminant, which Sigmund Freud postulated is of little worth:

> ... readiness for a universal love of mankind and the world represents the highest standpoint which man can reach. ...I should like to bring forward my two main objections to this view. A love that does not discriminate seems to me to forfeit a part of its own

value, by doing an injustice to its own object; and secondly, not all men are worthy of love (1989, p. 66).

Simone Weil

Simone Weil is as difficult to classify as she is to characterize. Three-quarters of a century after her death she is variously referred to as a philosopher, social activist, philanthropist, Marxist, religious seeker, and Christian mystic. T.S. Eliot remembered her as "a woman of genius, of a kind of genius akin to that of saints" (Liukkonen and Pesonen, 2010). Born in 1909 into a privileged family in Paris, she mastered Greek by age twelve and Sanskrit shortly thereafter as part of her unrelenting determination to study and understand the world she inhabited. Weil placed first in the entrance examination to the prestigious Ecole Normal Superieure in Paris. (Another embryonic genius, Simone de Beavior, who would later distinguish herself as an existential philosopher and metaphysical novelist, placed second.)

Weil displayed uncommon sensitivity to the plight of others as early as age six when she refused sugar in sympathy with French soldiers fighting on the Western Front in World War I. At 16 she identified with the working class and declared herself a Bolshevist and trade unionist. She frequently shared her salary with the unemployed. In 1934, in spite of her frail health, she took a leave of absence from teaching philosophy to work in a factory to intensify her protest of the exploitation of laborers. She disdained the ivory tower refuge of academia, believing a life isolated from manual labor and its suffering would disable her for meaningful teaching and writing. In this vein she wrote: "The intelligent man who is proud of his intelligence is like the condemned man who is proud of his cell"(2010). Her death at age 34 was attributed to a combination of tuberculosis, refusal of medical treatment, and physical neglect that included periods of starvation during political protests.

Her spiritual journey accelerated six years before her death when in Italy in the same church in which Saint Francis of Assisi prayed, she had a spiritual encounter. This experience had the life-changing effect described by William James in *The Varieties of Religious Experience* (1902). Previous to her epiphany, Weil's world view was secular and agnostic, if not atheistic. Following this experience, she measured life from a sacred, theological perspective. This radical reorientation fit James' characterization of an authentic religious conversion as an experience originating outside of the individual. He maintained religious conversions are not a mere reworking of ideas already held. If such were the case, the experience simply would be an intellectual exercise. Rather, the psychology of religious conversion requires the introduction and embracing of ideas totally foreign to the one receiving them. A purely psychological interpretation of Weil's conversion might explain it as the culmination of her frustration with the ineffectiveness of social and political institutions at significantly alleviating human suffering. Her conclusion, "From human beings, no help can be expected," implies her disillusionment with Marxism and suggests her realization that a radically different means for change was required (Liuukonen and Pesonen, 2010).

In David Foster Wallace's insightful meditation, *This Is Water*, he speaks of the unconscious error of incorrectly explaining phenomena in terms of existing presuppositions when the correct explanation might require reconsidering a previously rejected possibility (2009). Perhaps the explanation for Weil's conversion is not secular and psychological but to be found in the worldview she once dismissed. Perhaps, like Mother Teresa, she heard a voice from the spiritual realm that had the effect of redirecting her - perhaps the same voice heard by Albert Schweitzer.

Albert Schweitzer

Just as Mother Teresa has served a generation of baby-boomers as the paradigm of self-sacrificial human service, Albert Schweitzer did the same for the previous generation. The son of a Lutheran pastor, he distinguished himself throughout Europe as a musician and theological scholar by age 28. In 1896 he reflected on what he considered his life of privilege and made a decision about his future.

> One brilliant summer morning at Gunsbach, during the Whitsuntide holidays - it was in 1896 - as I awoke, the thought came to me that I must not accept this good fortune as a matter of course, but must give something in return. ... What the character of my future activities would be was not yet clear to me. I left it to chance to guide me. Only one thing was certain, that it must be direct human service, however inconspicuous its sphere (Schweitzer,1933, p. 82).

"From everyone who has been given much, much will be demanded; and from the one who has been entrusted with much, much more will be asked" (Luke 12:48). With these words Jesus commissioned his disciples. Schweitzer's gratitude for what he had received accounts for his resolution to spend the balance of his life giving. After committing himself to hands-on human service he became aware of the need for a physician in equatorial Africa. Upon learning of this need, he entered medical school at the University of Strasbourg in 1905 and graduated in 1912. He explained his determination to serve as a physician in terms of its contrast to his life as a scholar: "I wanted to be a doctor that I might be able to work without having to talk because for years I have been giving myself out in words (p. 82)."

Dr. Schweitzer's compassion and reverence for life encompassed all living things. He believed, "A man is truly ethical only when he obeys the compulsion to help all life he is able to assist, and shrinks from injuring anything that lives" (p. 235). An adherent to the Hindu principle of "nonviolence to all living things" (*ahimsa*), he admitted to ambivalence when choosing human life over that of a virus or tumor, since they too are life forms:

> I rejoice over the new remedies for sleeping sickness, which enable me to preserve life, where once I could only witness the progress of a painful disease. But every time I put the germs that cause the disease under the microscope I cannot but reflect that I have to sacrifice this life in order to save another. ... every day the responsibility to sacrifice one life for another caused me pain.
>
> Standing, as all living beings are, before this dilemma of the will to live, man is constantly forced to preserve his life and life in general only at the cost of other life. If he has been touched by the ethic of Reverence for Life, he injures and destroys life only under a necessity he cannot avoid, and never from thoughtlessness (p. 236).

Does Schweitzer's philosophical consistency constitute an obsession with life worthy of designation as a mental illness? He performed surgery neither annoyed nor distracted by the flies flitting about his operating room. Rare? Yes. Extreme? Of course. Sick? If so, why? Szasz would insist the absence of a universal understanding of how people *ought* to behave means Schweitzer is unlike most people and even eccentric, but not mentally ill. Freud, were he aware of Schweitzer's regard for life, would have questioned his philosophy if not his mental health. As previously stated, "A love that does not discriminate ... (forfeits) a part of its own value, by doing an injustice to its object "(1989, p. 66).

Albert Lexie

Albert Lexie has donated over $220,000 to the Free Care Fund of Children's Hospital in Pittsburgh, Pennsylvania. While this amount is impressive, what makes it amazing is that he earned only $10,000 a year shining shoes. The $220,000 came from the tips he accumulated over 35 years before retiring in 2017. The Free Care Fund is for children whose families cannot afford their medical care. A beloved figure at the hospital, he has been recognized by several organizations for his philanthropy and featured in several stories, including a biography, *Albert's Kids: The Heroic Work of Shining Shoes for Sick Children* (Rouvalis and Maurer, 2012).

The Question

This chapter began with a question: *Is it possible to be pathologically good?* Alternatively stated, is there a degree of love for humanity that can be explained only as a manifestation of a mental illness? To this point, Zell Kravinsky, Simone Weil, Albert Schweitzer, and Albert Lexie have been considered. Each is known for a life of charity. On what basis might it be concluded that the noteworthy life of any or all of them is attributable to a psychological disorder?

The altruistic lives of these individuals, while extraordinary, are not identical. The sacrifices of Kravinsky, Schweitzer, and Lexie provided benefits for others. The same cannot be said of Weil's self-denial. Except for the few unemployed recipients of Weil's money and those students who might have been inspired by her compassion, her lifestyle provided no tangible advantage for others. Further, her asceticism deprived her family of a daughter and sister. Weil's neglect of her well-being is reminiscent of Dostoevsky's Lise in *The Brothers Karamazov*:

> (Lise) unlocked the door, opened it a little, put her finger in the crack, and slammed the door as hard as she could. Ten seconds later she released her hand, went slowly to the chair, sat down, and looked intently at her blackened, swollen finger and the blood that was oozing out from under the nail. her lip quivered.
> "I'm a vile, vile, vile, despicable creature," she whispered. (1970, p. 703).

Like Lise, Weil's self-inflicted suffering had no effect beyond herself.

Although Kravinsky helped others, he also gave at the expense of his family. He deprived his wife and children of great wealth. The question of whether millions of dollars would have provided a better life for them is not at issue. The reality is he decided to remove this advantage from his family and distribute it to others. What is certain is, at one point, he was prepared to deprive his family of a husband and father. Reflecting on his philanthropy, Kravinky offers this explanation:

> I do not feel I am crazy, I am looking for the moral life. This means I cannot have wealth, or the use of two kidneys, when others have none. I cannot value myself and my life higher than others. I feel better for giving everything, whether it is my money or my body. Sometimes I feel that the moral life is so close now, I can almost touch it (Laurence, 2004).

Unlike Kravinsky and Weil, the benevolence of Schweitzer and Lexie came at no cost to anyone. Even Ayn

Rand would have recognized this difference and characterized Kravinsky and Weil as more concerned with how to die rather than how to live (1961, 49). Whatever their differences, the love for humanity demonstrated by these four people is rare indeed. Szasz believed the difference between admirable and derisive philanthropy is the persuasion of other people:

> In proportion as we succeed in persuading them, we can become accredited as moral leaders: Tolstoy and Gandhi were eminently successful at this. In proportion as we fail in persuading them, we become defined as mad fanatics (1973, p. 48).

For Elton Trueblood, love for humanity is an expression of the meaning of life:

> Man is so made that he cannot find genuine satisfaction unless his life is transcendent in at least two ways. It must transcend his own ego in that he cares more for a cause than for his own existence, and it must transcend his own brief time in that he builds for a time when he is gone and thereby denies mortality. A man has at least made a start on discovering the true meaning of life when he plants shade trees under which he knows full well he will never sit (1951, pp. 57-58).

XII. Heroism as Spirituality and Transcendence

God did not call me to be successful, He called me to be obedient.

Mother Teresa

Although the eye beholds rocks, mountains, trees, and sky, this is only a veil drawn over a vast, mysterious unseen reality.

Deepak Chopra

Shortly before his death, baseball legend Lou Gehrig said, "I consider myself the luckiest man on the face of the earth" (2017). But it was a baseball player of less renown, Jack Lohrke, who had the nickname "Lucky." According to his son, John, "He really didn't like that nickname. It reminded him of too many things." Jack Lohrke didn't like being reminded of his several brushes with death.

"Because I could not stop for death, he kindly stopped for me," wrote Emily Dickinson (1924). Finally, at age 85, two days after suffering a stroke, death stopped for Jack Lohrke. A World War II veteran, he fought at Normandy and the Battle of the Bulge and emerged unscathed. Four times a soldier next to him was killed. He didn't consider himself a hero ("I wasn't exactly Sgt. York") any more than he considered himself lucky ("The name is Jack, Jack Lohrke") (Fimrite, 1994).

Returning home in 1945, he was bumped from a transport flight at the last minute. The plane crashed, killing everyone on board. The following year, having resumed his baseball career, Lohrke was traveling by bus in Washington State with a Class B minor league team, the Spokane Indians. During a stop for food, he was told he had been promoted to Triple A, so he took his gear and hitchhiked to Spokane. A few hours later the Indians' bus crashed into a canyon, killing nine of his former teammates.

Lohrke went on to a seven-year major league career with the New York Giants and Philadelphia Phillies, retiring with a career batting average of .242 and 22 home runs. He appeared as a pinch hitter in the 1951 World Series. Still, he is best remembered for surviving a war and two crashes that could have taken his life.

Fate is an irresistible power believed to control events. Luck is the unknown and unknowable means by which events happen. Is there a power that controls events and was Jack Lohrke favored by this power? If so, is the reason for his favor discoverable? Or was it luck?

Sociologist Peter Berger has written, "If commentators on the contemporary situation of religion agree about anything, it is that the supernatural has departed from the modern world" (1969, p. 1). Notwithstanding, as implied by the title of his book, *A Rumor of Angels*, Berger believes a widespread fascination for the supernatural persists even in the current scientific age. Evidence of this fascination is the popularity of the movie, "The Sixth Sense" (Shyamalan, 1999). Its ticket sales exceeded production costs by $630,000,000 and it was America's number one box office attraction for five weeks in 1999. The story of an eight-year-old boy who has the ability to peer into another dimension of reality and see dead people, this movie's success is inexplicable apart from a widespread curiosity about preternatural activity. This same curiosity accounts for the immense popularity of Stephen King's novelistic excursions into a world that might be. Neurosurgeon Eben Alexander's memoir, *Proof of Heaven*, recounting his near-death experience, rose to the top of *The New York Times* paperback best-seller list immediately upon its publication (2012). Moreover, the popularity of astrology, which has no relationship with the science of astronomy, tarot card readings, seances, mediums, and other psychic activities provide additional support for Berger's assertion that there is "a rumor of angels" among us.

The distinguished historian and philosopher Mircea Eliade believed human beings are hardwired for belief in the supernatural and employed the term *homo religiosus* (religious man) to characterize this disposition. In his classic, *The Sacred and the Profane*, he posited all people, including those who claim to be exclusively secular in their worldview, are sometimes unconsciously attracted to sacred behaviors and beliefs (1987).

Are human beings naturally disposed to pursue some form of faith in and worship of a supreme being? The celebrated humorist Will Rogers wryly said of himself, "I am not a member of any organized political party, I'm a democrat" (2012). Similarly, many people characterize themselves as "not religious, but spiritual." Like Rogers, such people have an interest without institutional membership. To be spiritual means to be *dualistic* - to believe there are two dimensions of reality, one physical and accessible by means of the senses; the other nonphysical and imperceptible to the senses. "Spirituality is a process that leads us on a journey from the seen to the unseen, the visible to the invisible dimension of human existence" (Ponomareff and Bryson, 2006, p. 89). Albert Einstein made a spiritual reference in a letter he wrote to a sixth grader who had written to ask if scientists pray. Einstein's response included this observation:

> … everyone who is seriously involved in the pursuit of science becomes convinced that a spirit is manifest in the laws of the Universe – a spirit vastly superior to that of man and in the face of which we with our modest powers must feel humble (Calaprice, 2002, p. 129).

To transcend means to rise above or go beyond the limits of something. Transcendence is not synonymous with spirituality, but the latter can empower the former. The individuals featured in the balance of this chapter had a spiritual perspective on life that enabled them to rise above mundane considerations and take action that was counter to their earthly interests. (The previous sentence was written in the past tense since all of them are deceased except for Andrea Jaeger.) William James defined religion as "the attempt to live in harmony with an unseen order of things" (2017). Given this definition, it is accurate to characterize all of them as religious.

The spirituality and transcendence of Dietrich Bonhoeffer (Chapter II), Eric Liddell (Chapters IX and X), and Albert Schweitzer (Chapter XI) have been addressed previously. Concerning Bonhoeffer, the German pastor and theologian who actively opposed the Nazi regime, it is widely believed his participation in the German resistance movement included involvement in a plot to assassinate Adolf Hitler. Bonhoeffer believed a failure to take direct action against evil is tantamount to condoning it. Accordingly he wrote:

> If I sit next to a madman as he drives a car into a group of innocent bystanders. I can't, as a Christian, simply wait for the catastrophe, then comfort the wounded and bury the dead. I must try to wrestle the steering wheel out of the hands of the driver (2017).

It would strain the imagination to conceive of a more dangerous activity than publicly opposing Hitler and the Nazis while living in Germany in the 1940's. Bonhoeffer risked his safety and eventually gave his life for the cause in which he believed.

Thomas More, also referred to previously, (Chapter X), served King Henry VIII as Lord Chancellor of England until

More refused to endorse the king's intention to divorce Catherine of Aragon and marry Anne Boleyn. When Pope Clement VII refused to grant a marital annulment the king withdrew England from the Catholic Church and established the Church of England in its place. More refused to sign the Oath of Supremacy, which declared Henry as the head of the church. Eventually, More was convicted of treason, in spite of questionable testimony at his trial. Shortly before his execution by decapitation he is reputed to have said, "I die the king's good servant but God's first" (Monti, 1997, p. 449).

Few people wear as many hats successfully as did Andrew Greeley: Roman Catholic priest, sociologist, professor, journalist, and bestselling novelist. In his variety of engagements, Father Greeley showed an unflinching willingness to address sensitive issues, always with kindness and clarity.

Most Catholic priests live honorable lives of service, subordinating fleshly desires to their calling of human service on behalf of God. Like Father Greeley, they provide a contrast to the minority of priests whose moral failures have been well publicized. In a refreshingly honest essay, "Of Course Priests Fall in Love," he explains the spirituality and transcendence of priests who have chosen a life many people find unfathomable.

> Celibacy does not mean that one does not fall in love or love; it rather means that one has made other commitments of such importance that one does not end up in bed with those one loves. Married men and women also fall in love; frequently it is with their spouse with whom they fall in love ... . But other times their loves, often sudden and transient, often profound and durable, are not their spouses. Yet infidelity usually does not occur and indeed is unthinkable because the basic commitments of their lives are

richer, more important and more rewarding. To pretend that such reactions do not occur is absurd. To pretend that they are not possible is cynical and ugly.

One of the principle reasons for having celibates in a community is to have living proof that intense human emotional attractions need not end up in the bedroom and indeed need not even present a serious threat of doing so.

So, yeah, I have been in love often, sometimes for many years. Yet I have other commitments which are not really disturbed by such love and in fact are probably strengthened.

Are the persons who so attract me unappealing as bed partners? Heavens no, they grow more appealing through the years and the decades (an interesting discovery, by the way). Has the fact that they are not bed partners and won't be caused some frustration? Well, yes, but then the opposite outcome would have produced its own variety of frustrations, as married people will surely testify. All love has its frustrations and its rewards.

The point is, however, that there is a wide variety of possible loves available to humans, all of them with their own rewards, challenges, excitements, frustrations and disappointments. We cannot have them all, we must pick and choose (1983, pp. 129-131).

In 1981, at age 16, Andrea Jaeger was the second ranked women's professional tennis player in the world. Six years later she retired from tennis and moved to Aspen, Colorado with $1.4 million she had won on the tour and founded the Little Star Foundation, devoted to programs for seriously ill, abused or at-risk children. In 2006 she made another significant life change when she became Sister Andrea, an Anglican Dominican nun.

Often she has been asked if she misses tennis and thinks about the career she might have had if she had not retired at 23. "No regrets, " has been her response, "God wanted me to do something else, and it happened to be helping children with cancer. I love what I do" (Bane, 2006). She is reminiscent of the Christian martyr Jim Eliot who wrote, "No man is a fool who gives up what he cannot keep to gain that which he cannot lose" (2017).

Conclusion: Two Philosophers Discuss Spirituality and Transcendence

It can be informative as well as entertaining to imagine a conversation that never took place. Such a conversation is Bertrand Russell (1872-1970) and Gottfried Liebniz (1646-1716) meeting for an anachronistic lunch to discuss the existence of God in the light of evil and suffering. Russell, although he admitted he could not disprove God's existence, characterized himself as an atheist. Liebniz, a man of faith, not only believed in God, but believed God to be omnipotent and benevolent.

In their conversation Russell would express a secular, mundane perspective and Liebniz a spiritual, transcendent view. Given the literature each produced, their conversation would likely produce the following dialogue:

Russell: Gottfried, how is it possible a brilliant man like you believes God exists?
Liebniz: Bertrand, I think I know where you're going with that question. So rather than me answering it, why not proceed to say what you have on your mind?
Russell: Very well, Gottfried. A benevolent and omnipotent God cannot be reconciled with the evil and suffering in this

world. Evil and suffering in this world is undeniable, which makes the existence of God an impossibility.

Liebniz: Much of the evil and suffering in this world is the result of human free will. There are many people who choose to act in ways that bring suffering to others.

Russell: I knew the "free will argument" was coming. I'll concede that free will accounts for a great deal of misery. But earthquakes, cancers, hurricanes, viruses, and birth defects do not involve any human agency. Surely an omniscient God would be aware of these evils as well and, if loving and all-powerful, would not tolerate them.

Liebniz: Bertrand, just as you anticipated one of my arguments I've anticipated yours. I'm not naive to the nonhuman induced suffering in this world. What I believe is this world, with all its imperfections and tragedies, is the best possible world.

Russell: Have you taken leave of your senses? Are you saying this world of calamities and ineffable suffering is perfect?

Liebniz: No, not perfect, but the best possible world given the circumstances.

Russell: Given the circumstances? I can't imagine the circumstances that would justify the world in which we live.

Liebniz: Precisely, Bertrand, you can't imagine the circumstances and neither can I. The allowance of evil and suffering is part of the long range plan God has for the entire creation.

Russell: I can't imagine any long range plan that would make sense of the pain and ugliness of this world. This is beyond my comprehension.

Liebniz: Excellent, Bertrand! You've located the problem. Given our limited intellect and tiny place in the history of the universe we are incapable of understanding God's plan for the creation. If we could grasp His plan we would comprehend the rationale for evil and suffering.

Russell: I think you've constructed an intellectual argument to support your emotional need to believe in a loving, omnipotent God.

Liebniz: And I could say the same to you - that you've rationalized not believing in God because of an emotional need to be an atheist. Bertrand, can you locate a flaw in this sequence of thought?

1. God conceptualized an infinite number of universes.
2. Only one universe was brought into existence.
3. God's choices are subject to the principle of sufficient reason, meaning God has an adequate reason for choosing one thing over another.
4. God is good.
5. Therefore, the universe that God chose to create is the best possible universe, which includes this world.

Russell: Gottfried, as you well know, people often argue correctly from incorrect premises. Your sequence of thought is logical but assumes the existence of God. You're begging the question under consideration.

Liebniz: And you're not? Doesn't your position that evil and suffering prove God's nonexistence arise from the premise that God does not exist.

Russell: I don't claim to have disproven God's existence. What I do claim, as I presented in one of my lectures, is,

it is a most astonishing thing that people can believe that this world, with all the things that are in it, with all its defects, should be the best that omnipotence and omniscience has been able to produce in millions of years. I really cannot believe it. Do you think that, if you were granted omnipotence and omniscience and millions of years in which to perfect your world, you could produce nothing better than the Ku-Klux-Klan or the Fascists? (1927).

Leibniz: I believe another lunch is in order to pursue this matter further.

Russell: Finally, we have agreed upon something. Guten tag, Gottfreid.

XIII. Heroism as Redemption

He picked up the lemons that Fate had sent him and started a lemonade stand.

Elbert Hubbard

Andy Dufresne, Stephen King's protagonist in *Rita Hayworth and Shawshank Redemption* (1982), is a literary illustration of redemption. Sentenced to life imprisonment for a murder he did not commit, Dufresne made the most of his incarceration. He upgraded the prison library, tutored a fellow inmate for a high school diploma, provided tax consultations for prison employees, and accomplished a 17-year plan for his escape. Indeed, Dufresne made the most of his time in Shawshank, which is to say he *redeemed* his imprisonment.

Redemption can take any one of three expressions:

-making something tolerable
-finding or creating something good in a bad situation
-atoning or compensating for a misdeed

Making Something Tolerable

Andy Dufresne is fictional, Viktor Frankl is not. Frankl, a psychiatrist, was imprisoned for three years in Nazi concentration camps. After his liberation he wrote *Man's Search for Meaning* (1959), a classic in both psychology and philosophy. His motivation for writing was unambiguously redemptive:

I had wanted to simply convey to the reader by way of a concrete example that life holds a potential meaning under any conditions, even the most miserable ones.

And I thought that if the point were demonstrated in a situation as extreme as a concentration camp, my book might gain a hearing. I therefore felt responsible for writing down what I had gone through, for I thought it might be helpful to people who are prone to despair (1959, p. 16).

The epilogue to his book has an unmistakable redemptive tone. Therein Frankl presents the concept of *tragic optimism* - his philosophy that life entails three unavoidable tragedies that can be redeemed. The tragedies are pain, guilt, and death. He explains the potential for optimism in the midst of tragedy with these words:

> ... what matters is to make the best of any given situation. "The best," however, is that which in Latin is called *optimum* - hence the reason I speak of tragic optimism, that is, an optimism in the face of tragedy and in view of the human potential which at its best always allows for: (1) turning suffering into a human achievement and accomplishment; (2) deriving from guilt the opportunity to change oneself for the better; and (3) deriving from life's transitoriness an incentive to take responsible action (p. 162).

Finding or Creating Something Good in a Bad Situation

Following the death of his son, the philosopher Nicholas Wolterstorff wrote:

> It's so wrong, so profoundly wrong, for a child to die before its parents. It's hard enough to bury our parents. But that we expect. Our parents belong to our past, our children belong to our future (1987, p. 16).

Kevin and Kristie Shroyer know what it is to bury a child. Their daughter, Korinne, mired in a clinical depression, committed suicide at age 14. Her death, literally, saved the life of a 43-year-old man. In the week following Korinne's suicide her parents

> ... decided to send out her organs like gifts.
> Her green eyes would go in one direction, her glad heart another, her kidneys still another. Her liver and her pancreas went somewhere else, and her two good lungs - the ones that played the saxophone - went to a Gainsville, Georgia man named Len Geiger, who was so close to dying that he was practically pricing caskets (Reilly, 2007).

In 2002 Kevin Shroyer and Len Geiger ran in an 8K race together; something Geiger could not have done were it not for Korinne's lungs. Eventually Geiger married and became the father of a daughter, Ava Corinne, named after the girl whose gift extended his life.

Rabbi Harold Kushner also lost a 14-year-old child. His son, Aaron, died of progeria, the rare disease that accelerates the aging process. At the time of his death Aaron Kushner had the anatomy and physiology of a 90-year-old man. Understandably, Rabbi Kushner required a leave-of-absence from his work to grieve and consider his future. He wondered if he could serve his congregation as their rabbi when he had questions about his own faith. During his sabbatical he wrote *When Bad Things Happen to Good People* (1981), a bestseller and now a classic in the field of pastoral care and counseling. Like the Shroyers, Rabbi Kushner produced something good from a heartbreaking loss.

Atoning or Compensating for a Misdeed

The playwright Tennessee Williams wrote, "Hell is yourself and the only redemption is when a person puts himself aside to feel deeply for another person" (2017). In the movie "Seven Pounds" Will Smith's character, Ben Thomas, glances at his cell phone while driving, loses control of his car, and causes an accident in which seven people are killed. After the accident his brother is diagnosed with lung cancer and in need of a transplant. When Ben donates one of his lungs it occurs to him that he might atone for the accident by making other donations. He then seeks out six people in need of organs and makes other donations. (The last two donations, corneal and heart, came after his suicide.)

Another playwright, Oscar Wilde, observed, "No man is rich enough to buy back his past" (2017). While this is true, it does not preclude some people from trying to make atonement. The legendary boxing champion Muhammed Ali regretted his prodigious womanizing as a young man and endeavored to live honorably in his later years. His biography includes this reflection:

> I used to chase women all the time. And I won't say it was right, but look at all the temptations I had. I was young, handsome, heavyweight champion of the world. Women were always offering themselves to me. I had two children by women I wasn't married to. I love them; they're my children. I feel just as good and proud of them as I do my other children, but it wasn't the right thing to do. And running around, living that kind of life, wasn't good for me. It hurt my wife, it offended God. It never really made me happy. But ask any man who's forty years old – if he knew at twenty what he knows now, would he do things different? Most people would. So I did wrong; I'm sorry. And all I'll say as far as running around chasing women is

concerned, is that's all past. I've got a good wife now, and I'm lucky to have her (Hauser, 1991, p. 310).

In contrast to his years of self-indulgence, Ali came to believe, "Service to others is the rent you pay for your room here on earth" (2017). He also believed, "I've made my share of mistakes along the way, but if I have changed even one life for the better, I haven't lived in vain" (2017). Like Ali, Charles Colson regretted his earlier life and made a commitment to bring honor to God through human service. Once known as President Nixon's "hatchet man" and an "evil genius," Colson was involved in the infamous Watergate break-in and served seven months in a federal prison for obstruction of justice. The year before his incarceration he embraced Christianity and radically reordered his life. Thirty years later *Time* magazine recognized him as one of the 25 most influential evangelical Christians in America (2005). He founded several non-profit Christian ministries, including the Prison Fellowship and the Prison Fellowship International. Before his death in 2012 he had received 15 honorary doctorates, a Templeton Prize for Progress in Religion (awarded for an exceptional contribution to affirming a spiritual worldview), and a Presidential Citizens Medal. He donated the one million dollar Templeton Prize, royalties from his 30 books, and all his speaker's fees to the Prison Fellowship ministry.

The quotation introducing this chapter was written as part of an obituary for the actor, humorist, and artist Marshall Wilder, a dwarf with severe curvature of the spine (kyphosis). Shortly after his death it was written of him, "Wilder coaxed the frown of adverse fortune into a smile" (The Oakland Tribune, 02/06/1915).

XIV. Heroism as Self-Knowledge and Change

Note: This chapter is written in the first person since the topic applies to us all. In addition, writing from the "I/we" point-of-view makes for an easier read.

The final mystery is oneself.

Oscar Wilde

The hardest road to travel is the one that leads a man to himself.

Herman Hesse

Inscribed in the forecourt of the Temple of Apollo at Delphi is *gnothi seauton* (know thyself). The same injunction serves as the motto of Hamilton College, a prestigious Upstate New York school. Saint Augustine prayed, "O God, I pray you let me know myself" (2009). Shakespeare's Polonius advised his son Laertes, "to thine own self be true," albeit without telling him how to identify his true self. (*Hamlet*, 1.3.78). Highly regarded among mental health professionals is *The Search for the Real Self*, written by a psychiatrist, James Masterson (1988). And another psychiatrist, Thomas Szasz, expressed disagreement with Masterson when he asserted, "People often say that this or that person has not yet found himself. But the self is not something one finds; it is something one creates" (1973, p. 49).

Philosophical novelist Walker Percy posited knowledge of the self is not easily attained: "Why is it that of all the billions and billions of strange objects in the cosmos – novas, pulsars, black holes – you are beyond doubt the strangest?" (1984, p.

7). Nietzsche went further, stating that self-knowledge is an impossibility: "We are unknown, we knowers, to ourselves ... each of us holds good to all eternity the motto: 'Each of us is farthest away from himself' - as far as ourselves are concerned we are not knowers" (2003, p. 1). The poet Robert Burns suggested an understanding of how we appear to others requires divine empowerment: "O would some Power, the gift to give us, to see ourselves as others see us" (1786).

What makes you uniquely you and me uniquely me? By what means do we arrive at a sense of self? What does it mean when we say, "I am not myself today" or, "You don't seem like yourself"? Why is self-knowledge important to us and what are the implications of not having it?

As previously noted, there are 17,953 personality traits (Allport and Odbert, 1936). According to Freud, our minds operate at three levels: conscious, subconscious, and unconscious. Given the complexity of our composition and operation a complete and impeccable self-knowledge is impossible. Nevertheless, we can know ourselves substantially since there are at least seven sources for self-knowledge.

1. *Psychological Testing*: Personality instruments like the MMPI and Meyers-Briggs Type Inventory and projective tests like the TAT and Rorschach Ink Blot Test have a high level of validity among mental health professionals.
2. *Convergent Data*: When two or more people who have no connection with each other make the same observation about us it is likely an accurate estimation.
3. *Continuity of Behavior*: Simply stated, we are who we are most of the time. We are not defined by a rare, out-of-character behavior.
4. *Accomplishments*: Our achievements demonstrate certain characteristics. For example, losing 50 pounds

by maintaining a diet and exercise program is irrefutable evidence of self-discipline.

5. *Anonymity*: A charitable act performed anonymously demonstrates benevolence; an immoral act not performed when discovery was impossible demonstrates integrity.

6. *Desire*: Thomas Merton wrote, "We are made in the image of what we desire" (2009). The sacrifices we make in order to acquire or achieve are self-revealing.

7. *Significant Decisions*: Often, important decisions are difficult to make. How we decide and what we decide provide information about ourselves to ourselves.

Self-Knowledge and Change

In contrast to lawyers, psychiatrists have to tolerate few jokes about their profession. One of the few is this "light bulb" joke:

Question: How many psychiatrists does it take to change a light bulb?
Answer: Only one, but the light bulb has to really want to change.

Unlike a light bulb, we sometimes want to change. But change requires an honest self-assessment - something that can be an unsettling experience. An unflinching self-examination requires courage and change, which rarely comes easily, requires persistence. This combination of courage and persistence qualify self-knowledge and change as expressions of heroism.

But do we have the ability to change ourselves? An Italian proverb teaches, "Quando una persona fu nato rotondo, non puoi morire quadrata." (Translated to English as, "When a person is born round, he doesn't die square.") If this proverb is correct, any effort at significant change is a fool's errand.

Of course, we can change our bodies through diet and exercise. Cosmetic surgery also makes physical change possible, albeit expensively. The American Society for Aesthetic Plastic Surgery reported 15.9 million cosmetic surgical and nonsurgical procedures in 2014 (ASAPC, 2014). While change through diet and exercise requires self-discipline and perseverance, the same is not true for cosmetic surgery. This being said, this chapter is not concerned with bodily changes but changes in personality traits and targeted behaviors.

Synonyms for *change* include *alter, vary, modify, transform,* and *convert. Rehabilitate* is not usually synonymous with change, but the two words are equivalent in the context of a scene from the movie "The Shawshank Redemption" (1994). (Adapted from the Stephen King novella referred to in the previous chapter.) In the scene, at a parole hearing, a convicted murderer is asked, "Are you rehabilitated?" The convict, Ellis Boyd Redding, a man who has served 40 years of a life sentence, recognizes the question as tantamount to being asked, "Have you changed?" His eloquent response satisfies the parole board that he is, indeed, a different man. This kind of change constitutes a substantial change in personality - "an individual's characteristic pattern of thinking, feeling, and acting" (Myers, 2011, p. 553). Such change is rare, but not limited to fictional characters. Recall Charles Colson's change as described in Chapter XIII (Heroism and Redemption). T.S. Eliot wrote, "One starts an action simply because one must do something" (Wholey, 1998, p. 6). This observation describes the nadir in Laura Baugh's life. A professional golfer and alcoholic, in 1996, at age 41, she was taken to the hospital with spontaneous bleeding (thrombocytopenia) caused by an alcohol induced reduction of platelets (the blood component necessary for clotting). When she was told by a physician that her next drink would be fatal, she resolved to do something. Confronted with imminent death, she entered the Betty Ford Clinic and has maintained sobriety to the present. Her change is more than the mere elimination of a single behavior. Her sobriety required a radical reordering of her life. Her readjusted priorities have taken her from daily drunkenness to exemplary motherhood. Her autobiography, *Out of the Rough*, is a story of heroic self-admission and change (1999).

Dr. Ed Rosenbaum's memoir, *A Taste of My Own Medicine: When the Doctor Is the Patient*, tells a similar story. It recounts the diagnosis and treatment of his laryngeal cancer (1988). Frightened by the seriousness of his condition and dehumanized by the medical personnel who treated him, a significant change in his style of relating to his patients emerged. When he returned to his practice after successful treatment, his newfound empathy for the gravely ill made him an empathic patient advocate and physician-teacher. This was a pronounced contrast to his previous manner. Said Jim Rosenbaum upon the passing of his father, "He left a legacy and changed the way physicians practice," (Beaven, 2009).

XV. Heroism in Facing Death

When your time comes to die, be not like those whose hearts are filled with fear of death, so that when their time comes they weep and pray for a little more time to live their lives over again in a different way. Sing your death song, and die like a hero going home.

-Tecumseh

Heroes are admired for their courage, outstanding achievements, and/or noble qualities. We are fascinated and inspired by heroes because they remind us of our own potential. Recall this thought from Eric Hoffer, quoted in chapter I, "Can it be that even in the least of us there are crumbs of abilities and potentialities so that we can comprehend greatness as if it were a part of our own?" (2006, p. 82). Also recall that heroes encourage us to believe that even if God does not exist, the world can be a less hostile and better place because of them.

This chapter recounts the stories of ten people who acted heroically when confronted with death. Each was an ordinary person in an extraordinary circumstance: a soldier, a college student, a pregnant woman, a journalist, a physician, a college professor, and four clergymen. Each faced the end of life admirably.

Sullivan Ballou

The Battle at Bull Run was the first major engagement of the Civil War. Sullivan Ballou, a Union officer from Rhode Island, wrote to his wife on the eve of the battle. In his letter he eloquently expressed a heroic commitment to the cause for which he would be fighting and, possibly, dying:

I have no misgivings about, or lack of confidence in, the cause in which I am engaged, and my courage does not halt or falter. ... And I am willing - perfectly willing - to lay down all my joys in this life, to help maintain this Government ...

And how hard it is for me to give up and burn to ashes the future years, when, God willing, we might still have lived and loved together, and seen our sons grow up to honorable manhood around us. ...

Sarah do not mourn me dead, think I am gone and wait for thee, for we shall meet again (Carroll, 1997, p. 111-112).

One week after writing his letter, Sullivan Ballou was one of 481 Union soldiers killed at the First Battle of Bull Run.

Brent Foster

The day before Thanksgiving in 1994 a 21-year-old Harvard University student named Brent Foster was told he had inoperable bone cancer spreading through his body. This was not his first experience with the disease. Eight years earlier Brent lost his left leg to cancer. (Undaunted, he went on to play high school basketball on a prosthetic leg.) He withdrew from Harvard in February of his sophomore year, unable to continue his studies. Three months later the university presented him the Peter Wilson Truly Remarkable Student Award.

On July 13, 1995 he died in his hometown Des Moines, Iowa. (Ironically, this was eight years to the day after the amputation.) Shortly before his death he wrote:

These were supposed to have best the best days of my life. Instead I am at the losing end of an eight-year battle with cancer. And although only twenty-one, my body has grown extremely weak and will soon fail me altogether. In fact, every breath has become a struggle. After a total of eleven surgeries, a year of chemotherapy, and a month of high dose radiation, the doctors can do no more.

This is not the end for me but just the beginning. I find the concluding words of C.S. Lewis' *Chronicles of Narnia* very fitting: "Now at last they were beginning Chapter One of the Great Story which no one on earth has read; which goes on forever in which every chapter is better than the one before (Monroe, 1996, pp. 130,132).

Three months after his death, approximately 80 friends and family gathered for a memorial service at Harvard to celebrate the life of Brent Foster (Class of '97). It was an occasion for recognizing his devotion to his faith and the courage he demonstrated when death was imminent.

Four Clergymen

"Altruism, or benevolence, is the consideration of others before oneself. It is the opposite of egoism, the quality of thinking or acting with only oneself and one's own interests in mind" (Malikow, 2008, p. 11). In *The Pursuit of Happiness*, psychologist David Myers provides a narrative of four men who died altruistically in World War II.

With Nazi submarines sinking ships faster than the Allied forces could replace them, the troop ship SS Dorchester steamed out of New York harbor with 904 men headed for Greenland. Among those leaving anxious families behind were four chaplains, Methodist preacher George Fox, Rabbi Alexander Goode, Catholic priest John Washington, and

Reformed Church minister Clark Polling. Some 150 miles from their destination, a U-456 caught the Dorchester in its cross hairs. Within moments of a torpedo's impact, reports Larry Elliot, stunned men were pouring out from their bunks as the ship began listing. With power cut off, the escort vessels, unaware of the unfolding tragedy, pushed on in the darkness. On board, chaos reigned as panicky men came up from the hold without life jackets and leaped into overcrowded lifeboats.

When the four chaplains made it up to the steeply sloping deck, they began guiding the men to their boat stations. They opened a storage locker, distributed life jackets, and coaxed the men over the side. In the icy, oily smeared water, Private William Bednar heard the chaplains preaching courage and found the strength to swim until he reached a life raft. Still on board, Grady Clark watched in awe as the chaplains handed out the last life jacket, and then, with ultimate selflessness, gave away their own. As Clark slipped into the waters he saw the chaplains standing – their arms linked – praying, in Latin, Hebrew, and English. Other men, now serene, joined them in a huddle as the Dorchester slid beneath the sea (1992, p. 196).

Clementina Geraci

One of several Greek words for love is *storge*, the natural flow of affection parents have for their children. It is an unconditional, committed love that motivates self-sacrifice. Clementina Geraci's decision on behalf of her son epitomizes *storge*. Under the headline, "Mother picks death to continue her life through son's birth," *The Washington Post* reported the story of her choice to forego the aggressive cancer treatment that might have saved her life but would have required an abortion (03/07/1995).

> Clementina Geraci, three months pregnant, made the decision of her life when doctors told her last spring that her breast cancer had spread She could fight the cancer aggressively and have an abortion, or she could take less hazardous cancer drugs and carry the baby to term. ... Geraci, known as Tina, died Monday, March 6, at Washington Hospital Center, where she had worked as a resident in obstetrics and gynecology. She was 34 (*The Washington Post*, 03/07/1995).

Being a physician, Dr. Geraci fully understood her treatment options and the inherent risk in the one she chose.

During most of her pregnancy, Geraci took taxol, which doctors thought would not harm Dylan (her son). She had to stop taking the drug during the seventh month of her pregnancy, and Dylan was born one month prematurely by a Caesarean section, during which doctors discovered cancer in her liver. She resumed treatment, but it was too late (03/07/1995).

Christopher Hitchens

There are some people who never remind you of anyone else. Christopher Hitchens was such a person. His *New York Times* obituary headline reads, "Christopher Hitchens, Polemicist Who Slashed All, Freely, Dies at 62" (Grimes, 2011). For four decades he unflinchingly expressed his views on celebrities, politics, religion, and social issues in essays, books, lectures, and debates with eloquence, insight, and wit.

When his death from esophageal cancer was inevitable he said, "In whatever kind of 'race' life may be, I have very abruptly become a finalist" (2011). In a 2010 television interview he expressed no regrets for a lifetime of heavy smoking and drinking.

> Writing is what's important to me, and anything that helps me do that - or enhances and prolongs and deepens and sometimes intensifies argument and conversation - is worth it to me. It impossible for me to imagine having my life without going to those parties, without having those late nights, without that second bottle (2011).

Hitchens' bestseller, *God Is Not Great: How Religion Poisons Everything*, articulated his unambiguous atheism and antipathy for organized religion (2007). When death was imminent, he was asked about the possibility of a deathbed conversion. He responded,

> The entity making such a remark might be a raving, terrified person whose cancer had spread to the brain. I can't guarantee that such an entity wouldn't make such a ridiculous remark, but no one recognizable as myself would ever make such a remark (2011).

Woody Allen claimed, "I'm not afraid of death, I just don't want to be there when it happens" (05/04/2016). Hitchens wrote, "I personally want to 'do' death in the active and not the passive and to be there to look it in the eye and be doing something when it comes for me" (2011). That he did, he was fully present until the end.

Paul Kalanithi

Dr. Paul Kalanithi wrote his memoir, *When Breath Becomes Air*, in the interspersed windows of opportunity his rapidly failing health allotted (2016). Determined to optimize the rest of his life, he committed himself to spending as much time as possible with friends and family, especially his wife, Lucy, and newborn daughter, Cady. In addition, while his health and energy were continuously declining, he pushed himself to complete the book that would be his final contribution to his profession and legacy to his family. Pondering what to say to a daughter too young to engage in conversation, he wrote:

> There is perhaps only one thing to say to this infant, who is all future, overlapping briefly with me, whose life, barring the improbable, is all but past.
> That message is simple.
> When you come to one of the many moments in life where you must give an account of yourself, provide a ledger of what you have been, and done, and meant to the world, do not, I pray, discount that you have filled a dying man's days with a sated joy, a joy unknown to me in all my prior years, a joy that does not hunger for more and more but rests, satisfied. In this time, right now, that is an enormous thing (2016, p. 199).

Kalanithi died eight months after Cady's birth and ten months before the publication of a book *The New York Times* reviewed and recommended with this endorsement: "Finishing this book and then forgetting about it is simply not an option" (2016).

Randy Pausch

In the fall of 2007 a 46-year-old Carnegie-Mellon University computer science professor was informed the pancreatic cancer with which he had been diagnosed eleven months earlier would bring an end to his life within a year.

The professor, Randy Pausch, father of three, determined that he would make the most of the rest of his life. His determination included a hypothetical lecture that became a reality and an inspiration to millions of people all over the world. "The Last Lecture: Really Achieving Your Childhood Dreams," was given at Carnegie-Mellon on September 18, 2007, ten months before his death.

Subsequently, the lecture became a YouTube phenomenon and later a bestselling book, translated into 46 languages. Pausch was hardly self-pitying about the proximity of his death. In the spirit of *carpe diem* he said, "I don't know how to not have fun. I'm dying and I'm having fun, and I'm going to keep having fun every day I've got left" (2007).

Conclusion

Sullivan Ballou exemplifies commitment to duty; Brent Foster and the four clergymen epitomize religious faith; Clementina Geraci personifies love; Christopher Hitchens demonstrates integrity, Paul Kalanithi expresses generosity, and Randy Pausch represents redemption. What factors prepared these ten people to face the end of life heroically? Most likely it was the life each of them lived prior to their confrontation with death. It has been said that crisis creates character. Actually, character is not forged in crisis. Crisis brings out the character that has been fostered over a lifetime.

References

Preface

Picoult, J. (2017). Recovered from www.azquotes.com /author/11649 - Jodi_Picoult on 11/19/2017.

Chapter I. What Is a Heroism and Why Do We Admire Heroes?

Allport, G.W. & Odbert, H.S. (1936). "Trait names: A psycho-lexical study." *Psychological Monographs: General and Applied,* 47, 171 - 220. (1, Whole No. 211).

American Heritage Dictionary. (1973). New York: American Heritage Publishing Company.

Barkley, C. www.brainyquotes.com. Recovered 12/25/10.

Baum, L.F. (2000). *The wizard of Oz: 100th anniversary edition.* New York: HarperCollins.

Brooks, D. (2015). *The road to character.* New York: Random House.

Bunnell, D. (1974). "Tin Man." America (recording group).

DeSteno, D. and Valdesolo, P. (2013). *Out of character: Surprising truths about the liar, cheat, sinner (and saint) lurking in all of us.* New York: Crown Publishing Group.

Hammond, A. & Bettis, J. (1988). "One Moment in Time." Houston, W. (recording artist).

Hartsock, D. "Couric & Company." CBSnews.com. May 10, 2010 (interview).

Hoffer, E. (1973). *Reflections on the human condition.* New York: Harper and Row.

Homer, (1998). *The iliad.* Fagles, R. (translator).New York: Penguin Classics.

Hugo, V. (1987). New York: Penguin Books: Signet Classic.

Jamison, K. (1995). *An unquiet mind.* New York: Random House.

Kennedy, J.F. (1957). *Profiles in courage.* New York: Harper Perennial Classics.

Kilpatrick, W. (1992). *Why Johnny can't tell right from wrong: Moral illiteracy and the case for moral education.* New York: Simon and Schuster.

Lehrer, J. "Are heroes born or can they be made?" *The Wall Street Journal.* 12/11/10.

Liddell, H. and Scott, R. (2017). A Greek-English lexicon. Recovered from www.perseus.tufts.edu/hopper /text?doc. on 07/19/2017.

Martin, M. (1986). *Everyday morality: An introduction to applied ethics.* Belmont, CA: Wadsworth Publishing Company.

Ralston, A. (2004). *Between a rock and a hard place.* New York: Atria Books.

Seligman, M. and Peterson, C. (2004). *Character strengths and virtues.* Oxford, UK: Oxford University Press.

Twain, M. (2015). Recovered from www.twainquotes.com on 08/10/2015.

Wheelock, C. (1910). *American education.* Volume XIV. Number 1. New York: New York Department of Education.

Chapter II: Heroism as Courage

Aristotle. (1984). *Nichomachean ethics* in the *Complete works of Aristotle.* Jonathan Barnes, editor. W.D. Ross, translator. Princeton, NJ: Princeton University Press.

Birsch, D. (2014). *Introduction to ethical theories: A procedural approach.* Long Grove, IL: Waveland Press, Inc.

Bonhoeffer, D. (1953). "Who am I?" *Letters and papers from prison.* New York: Touchstone.

Borgman, A. (1995). "Mother's decision puts life of unborn child first - in final days of cancer she made videotapes for son." *The Washington Post.* 03/13/95.

Brown, J. (1859). Recovered from http://www.historyisa weapon.com website on 08/19/15.

Burke, E. (2015). Recovered from http://www.brainyquote. com website on 08/14/15.

Congressional Medal of Honor website. Recovered 08/16/15.

"Courage under fire." (1996). 20th Century Fox.

Garrison, W. (1831). "To the public." *The Liberator*. 01/01/1831.

Kipling, R. (2015). Recovered from http://www.kipling society.co.uk/poems_if.htm on 11/19/2017.

Luther, M. (2009). *Off the record with Martin Luther: An original translation of table talks*. Charles Daudert, editor and translator. Kalamazoo, MI: Hansa-Hewlett.

Martin, M. (1989). *Everyday morality*. Belmont, CA: Wadsworth Publishing.

"Monty Python and the holy grail." (1975). National Film Trustee Company.

Paraddo, N. (2015). Recovered from http://www.goodreads. com/work/quotes on 08/24/15.

"The princess bride."(2001). Walt Disney Pictures.

Wallace, J. (1978). *Vices and virtues*. Ithaca, NY: Cornell University Press.

Wilson, H. (2015). Recovered from www.quotationspage. com/quote website on 08/17/15.

Chapter III. Heroism as Self-Discipline

Burns, O. (1984). *Cold sassy tree*. New York: Houghton - Mifflin Publishing.

Freud, S. (2017). Recovered from https://www.goodreads.com /work/quotes on 07/24/2017.

Goleman, D. (1996). *Emotional intelligence: Why it can matter more than iq*. New York: Random House.

_____. (2015). Recovered from http://www.brainyquote. com.quotes on 08/27/15.

King, S. (1982). "Rita Hayworth and Shawshank redemption." *Different seasons*. New York: Penguin Publishing Group.

Lombardi, V. (2015). Recovered from http://www.brainy quote.com.quotes on 08/27/15.

Peck, M. (1978). *The road less traveled: A new psychology of love, traditional values and spiritual growth.* New York: Simon and Schuster.

Rather, D. (2004). "I cheated because I could." "60 Minutes" interview broadcast on 06/20/04.

Sapolsky, R. (2004). *Why zebras don't get ulcers: The acclaimed guide to stress, stress-related diseases, and coping.* Third edition. New York: Henry Holt and Company.

Chapter IV. Heroism as Justice

ACLU. (2015). Recovered from the American Civil Liberties Union website on 09/13/2015.

Gisham, J. (1989). *A time to kill*. New York: Random House.

King, M. (1998). *The autobiography of Martin Luther King, Jr.* New York: Warner books.

_____. (1989). "A letter from Birmingham jail." *Ethics in America source reader.* Lisa H. Newton, Editor. Englewood Cliffs, NJ: Prentice Hall.

Robson, K. (1998). *A great and glorious game. Baseball writings of A. Bartlett Giamatti.* Chapel Hill, NC: Algonquin Books.

Thoreau, H. (2014). *Resistance to civil government.* Charleston, SC: CreateSpace Publishing.

WCVB - TV. Boston, MA. 10/30/2012.

Chapter V. Heroism as Wisdom

Camus, A. (1955). *The myth of Sisyphus and other essays.* New York: Vintage Books/Random House.

Frankl, V. (2006). *Man's search for meaning.* Boston, MA: Beacon Press.

Johnson, L. (2007). *Practical philosophy: The Greco-Roman moralists.* Chantilly, VA: The Teaching Company.

Jones, A. (2007). *The road he travelled: The revealing biography of M. Scott Peck.* London, UK: Rider Books.

Peck, S. (1995). *In search of stones.* New York: Hyperion Books.

Vesely, A. (2011). "Viktor and I." Laguna Niguel, CA: Noetic Films, Inc.

Wittgenstein, L. (1991). *Philosophical investigations.* Anscombe, G.E.M., translator. Oxford, UK: Wiley-Blackwell Publisher.

Chapter VI. Heroism as Integrity

Cannon, J (1951). *The New York Post.* October 26, 1951.

Folsom, B. (1997). "Joe Louis vs. the IRS." Mackinac Center for Public Policy. Posted 07/07/1997. Recovered from http://www.mackinac.org/article on 05/21/2006.

McRea, D. (2002). *Heroes without a country.* New York: Harper Collins.

Rogers, F. (1992). Boston University Commencement Address. Boston, MA.

Chapter VII. Heroism as Perseverance

Burroughs, A. (2016). "day tripping." *Psychology today.* September/October 2016.

Hartman, D. and Asbell, B. (1978). *White cane, white coat: The extraordinary odyssey of a blind physician.* New York: Simon and Schuster.

"King gimp." (2012). Hadary, S. and Whiteford, W., Producers. HBO.

Kushner, H. (1981). *When bad things happen to good people.* New York: Schoecken Press.

Leibs, A. (2009). "Cerebral palsy no barrier to art: Dan Kepplinger's paintings explore the experience of disability. Vancouver, BK: Suite 101.com. Com Media, Inc. August 4, 2009.

Montgomery, L. (2015). *Anne of green gables*. Charleston, SC: Creatspace Publishing.

"Rocky." (1976). United Artists: Chartoff-Winkler Productions.

"Rudy." (2000). Sony Pictures Home Entertainment.

Saks, E. (2007). *The center cannot hold: My journey through madness*. New York: Hyperion Books.

Seuss, D. (1957). *And to think I saw it on mulberry street*. New York: Random House.

"The Cinderella Man." (2005). Miramax Films.

Viorst, J. (1986). *Necessary losses: The loves, illusions, dependencies, and impossible expectations that all of us have to give up in order to grow*. New York: Simon and Schuster.

Whitman, W. (2017). "Song of the open road." Recovered from www.bartleby.com/236/119.html on 11/20/2017.

Whittier, J. (2013). "Maude Miller." Recovered from ThinkExist.com website on June 25, 2012.

VIII. Heroism as Resilience

Camus, A. (1952). "Return to Tipassa." Recovered from genius.com/Albert-camus-return-to-tipassa on August 21, 2017.

Cohen, R. (2004). *Blindsided: living a life above illness - a reluctant memoir*. New York: Harper - Collins.

Clark, F. (2010). "Rethinking happiness: Resilience." "This emotional life." PBS: Vulcan Productions.

Dostoevsky, F. (2017). Recovered from http://www.famous quotesandauthors.com/authors/fyodor_dostoevsky_quo tes/hotml on August 22, 2017.

Krauthammer, C. (2013). *Things that matter: Three decades of passions, pastimes, and politics*. New York: Crown Forum.

Lafave, K.O. (2010). "Life as a human." TED. 03/13/2010.

Livingston, G. (2004). *Too soon old, too late smart: Thirty true things you need to know*. New York: Marlow & Company.

McMahon, J. (2014). "Camillus woman, shot 5 years ago, builds a new life with a new face." *Syracuse Post Standard* October 24, 2014.

Mullins, A. (2009). "How my legs give me super powers." TED Conference. February 2009. Recovered from http://www.quotationspage.com/quotes/Aimee_Mullis on 05/31/2011.

Nietzsche, F. (1997). *Twilight of the idols or how to philosophize with a hammer.* Indianapolis, IN: Hackett Publishing Company, Inc.

Roy, T. and Swift, E. (1998). *Eleven seconds: A story of tragedy, courage, and triumph.* New York: Warner Books.

Shumaker, R. (2010). "Rethinking happiness: Resilience." "This emotional life." PBS: Vulcan Productions.

Taylor, D. (1986). *The myth of certainty: The reflective Christian and the risk of commitment.* Downers Grove, IL: InterVarsity Press.

Wicker, C. (1989). "The man sentenced to life." *Orlando Sentinel.* 05/29/1989.

IX. Heroism as Commitment and Sacrifice

Carroll, A. (Editor). (1997). *Letters of a nation: A collection of extraordinary American letters.* New York: Broadway Books.

Chua, A. (2011). *Battle hymn of the tiger mother.* New York: The Penguin Press.

Gilkey, L. (1966). *Shantung compound.* New York: HarperCollins Publishers.

Jamison, K. (1995). *An unquiet mind: A memoir of moods and madness.* New York: Random House.

Liddell, E. (2017). Recovered from http://www. azquotes.com/author/8848-Eric_Liddell on August 27, 2017.

X. Heroism in Conflicting Situations

Calley, W. (2015). "The trial of William Calley." Recovered from Wikipedia, January 2015.

Gay, P. (1989). *Freud: A life for our times*. New York: W.W. Norton Company.

Kyle, C. (2015). Recovered from Brainy Quote website on April 27, 2015.

Nix, D. (2009). "Long silent Calley speaks." Columbus, GA: Ledger Enquirer. August 21, 2009.

Oliner, S. (2003). *Do unto others: Extraordinary acts of ordinary people*. Boulder, CO: Westview Press.

Sartre, J.P. (1957). *Existentialism and human emotions*. New York: Citadel Press. Kensington Publishing Corporation.

Szasz, T. (1973). *The second sin*. New York: Doubleday.

XI. Heroism as Love for Humanity

Blackburn, V. (2011). "The challenge for the unbeliever." Scottish Journal of Theology, 64, 313-326. 08/2011.

Camus, A. (1948). *The plague*. New York: Alfred K. Knopf, Inc.

Chesterton, G.K. recovered from www.quote/quotes/839 on 10/21/2010.

Dostoevsky, F. (1970). *The brothers Karamazov,* translated A.H. MacAndrew (New York: Bantam, 1970).

Fagone, J. Philadelphia Magazine. 5/15/2006.

Freud, S. (1989). *Civilization and its discontents.* New York: W.W. Norton and Company.

Hornby, N. (2001). *How to be good.* New York: Riverhead Books.

James, W. (1907). "The present dilemma of philosophy." *Pragmatism.* New York: Longman Green and Company.

_____ (1902) *Varieties of religious experience.* New York: Touchstone Publishers.

Johnson, T.L. (2007). The Teaching Company. Chantilly, VA.

Laurence, C. (2004). "I feel better for giving everything - whether my money or my organs." *The Telegraph.* www.telegraph.com.uk/. 08/08/2004.

Liukkonen, P. and Pesonen, A. (2010). Creative Commons. recovered from kaupunginkipjasto.10/22/2010.

Rand, A. (1961). *The virtue of selfishness.* New York: Penguin Books.

Rouvalis, C. and Maurer, S. (2012). *Albert's kids: The heroic work of shining shoes for children*. Pittsburgh, PA: RedDog Books.

Schweitzer, A. (1933). *Out of my life and thought*. Baltimore, MD: Johns Hopkins University Press.

Singer, P. (2006). "What should a billionaire give?" <u>New York Times Magazine</u>. 12/17/2006.

Strom (2003) "Doner wants to give until it hurts." *New York Times News Service*. 08/17/2003.

Szasz, T. (1973). *The second sin*. Garden City, New York: Anchor Books.

Trueblood, D. (1951). *The life we prize*. New York: Harper and Brothers.

Wallace, D. (2009). *This is water*. New York: Little, Brown, and Company.

Wittgenstein, L (1922). *Tractatus Logico-Philosophicus (TLP)*, 1922, C. K. Ogden (trans.), London: Routledge & Kegan Paul. Originally published as "Logisch-Philosophische Abhandlung", in *Annalen der Naturphilosophische*, XIV (3/4), 1921.

XII. Heroism as Spirituality and Transcendence

Alexander, E. (2012). *Proof of heaven: A neurosurgeon's journey into the afterlife*. New York: Simon and Schuster.

Bane, V. (2006). "Tennis star Andrea Jaeger's new life as a nun." *People Magazine.* November 18, 2006.

Berger, P. (1969). *A rumor of angels: Modern society and the rediscovery of the supernatural.* New York: Doubleday and Company, Inc.

Bonhoeffer, D. (2017). Recovered from http://www.az quotes.com/author/1638-Dietrich_Bonhoeffer on 11/23/2017.

Calaprice, A. Editor. (2002). *Dear Professor Einstein: Albert Einstein's letters to and from children.* Amherst, NY: Promethius Books.

Dickinson, E. (1924). *The complete poems of Emily Dickenson.* Boston, MA: Brown, Little, and Company.

Eliade, M. (1987). *The sacred and profane: The nature of religion.* New York: Harcourt, Brace, and Jovanonich.

Eliot, J. (2017). Recovered from http://www.goodreads. com/quotes/2919 on September 23, 2017.

Fimrite, R. "O lucky man." *Sports Illustrated.* October 14, 1994.

Gehrig, L. (2017). Recovered from baseball.org/discover/lougherig-luckiest-man on 11/23/2017.

Greeley, A. (1983). *A piece of my mind ... on just about everything.* Garden City, NY: Doubleday & Company, Inc.

James, W. (2017). Recovered from www.azquotes. com/quote/606174 on September 7, 2017.

Monti, J. (1997). *The king's good servant, but God's first*. San Francisco, CA: Ignatius Press.

Ponomareff and Bryson (2006).*The curve of the sacred: An exploration of human spirituality*. Value Inquiry Book Series. Volume 178.

Rogers, W. (2012). Recovered from Brainy Quote website on June 19, 2012.

Russell, B. (1927). "Why I am not a Christian." Lecture delivered to the South London Branch of the National Secular Society at the Battersea Town Hall on March 6, 1927.

Shyamalan, M. (1999). "The sixth sense." Burbank, CA: Buena Vista Pictures.

XIII. Heroism as Redemption

Ali, M. (2017). Recovered from http://brainyquote. com/authors/muhammed_ali on October 12, 2017.

Frankl, V. (1959). *Man's search for meaning*. New York: Simon and Schuster, Inc.

Hauser, T. (1991). Muhammed Ali: His life and times. New York: Simon and Schuster.

King, S. (1982). *Rita Hayworth and shawshank redemption: Different seasons*. New York: Viking Press: Penguin Group.

Kushner, H. (1981). *When bad things happen to good people.* New York: Schocken Press.

Reilly, R. (2007). "Getting a second wind." *Sports Illustrated.* Tampa, FL: Time, Inc.

Time. (2005). "The 25 most influential evangelicals in America: Charles Colson." February 7, 2005.

Wilde, O. (2017). Recovered from http://www.brainyquote. com/quotes/oscarwilde106470.html on October 12, 2017.

Williams, T. (2017). Recovered from http://www.brainyquote. com/ketwords/hell/html on October 12, 2017.

Wolterstorff, N. (1987). *Lament for a son.* Grand Rapids, MI: W.B. Eerdman's Company.

XIV. Heroism as Self-Knowledge and Change

Allport, G.W. & Odbert, H.S. (1936). Trait-names: A psycho-lexical study. *Psychological Monographs: General and Applied*, 47, 171-220. (1, Whole No. 211).

ASAPS. (2014). Recovered from http://www.plastisurgery org./Documents/news-resources/statistics/resources/ statistics/2014 on 10/15/2017 .

Augustine. Recovered from Rev. Fr. Benedict Hughes, CMRI. Sermon: "Lord That I May Know Myself ..." CMRI Index. August 3, 2009.

Baugh, L. and Eubanks, S. (1999). *Life out of the rough: An intimate portrait of Laura Baugh and her sobering journey.* Nashville, TN: Rutledge Hill Press.

Beaven, S. (2009). "prominent author and doctor dies." Oregonlive. Retrieved on 10/15/2017.

Burns, R. (1786) "To a louse." verse 8.

Masterson, J. (1988). *The search for the real self: Unmasking the personality disorders of our age.* New York: The Free Press.

Merton, T. Recovered from: http://moonriver.spaces.live.com. August 3, 2009.

Myers, D. (2007). *Psychology.* New York: Worth Publishers.

Nietzsche, F. (2003). *On a geneaology of morals: A polemic.* Translated by Douglas Smith. London, UK: Oxford University Classics.

Percy, W. (1984). *Lost in the cosmos: The last self help book.* New York: Simon and Schuster.

Rosenbaum, E. (1988). *A taste of my own medicine: When a doctor is a patient.* New York: Random House.

"Shawshank redemption." (1994). Columbia Pictures: Castle Rock.

Szasz, T. (1973). *The second sin.* Garden City, NY: Anchor Press. Doubleday and Company.

Wholey, D. (1998). *The miracle of change: The path to self-development and spiritual growth.* New York: Simon and Schuster.

XV. Heroism Facing Death

Allen, W. Recovered from http.www.Goodreads.com /author/Allen on 05/04/2016.

Carroll, A. (Editor). (1997). *Letters of a nation: A collection of extraordinary American letters.* New York: Broadway Books.

Grimes, W. (2011). "Christopher Hitchens, polemicist who slashed all, freely, dies at 62." *The New York Times.* 12/16/2011.

Hitchens, C. (2007). *God is not great: How religion poisons everything.* New York: Twelve. Hatchett Book Group.

Hoffer, E. *Reflections on the human condition.* Titusville, NJ: Hopewell Publications.

Kalanithi, P. (2016). *When breath becomes air.* New York: Random House.

Malikow, M. (2008). *Profiles in character: Twenty-six stories that will instruct and inspire teenagers.* Lanham, MD: University Press of America.

Monroe, K. (Editor). (1996). *Finding God at Harvard: Spiritual journeys of thinking Christians.* Grand Rapids, MI: Zondervan Publishing House.

Myers, D. (1992). *The pursuit of happiness: Who is happy and why*. New York: William Morrow and Company.

Pausch, R. "The last lecture: Really achieving your childhood dreams." Lecture given at Carnegie-Mellon University on 09/18/2007.

The Washington Post. "Mother picks death to continue life through her son." 03/07/1995.

About the Author

Dr. Max Malikow is on the faculty of the Renee Crown Honors Program of Syracuse University and an Adjunct Assistant Professor of Philosophy at LeMoyne College. He earned his Master's degree from Gordon-Conwell Theological Seminary and doctorate from Boston University. The author or editor of fourteen previous books, he is a practicing psychotherapist in Syracuse, New York.

Made in the USA
Middletown, DE
01 September 2021

47428616R00086